COMPE

THE FABIAN SERIES

Series Editor   Ben Pimlott

COMPETITIVE
SOCIALISM

AUSTIN MITCHELL

UNWIN
PAPERBACKS

LONDON SYDNEY WELLINGTON

First published in paperback by Unwin ® Paperbacks, an imprint
of Unwin Hyman Limited in 1989

Unwin Hyman Limited
15/17 Broadwick Street
London W1V 1FP

Allen & Unwin Australia Pty Ltd
8 Napier Street, North Sydney, NSW 2060, Australia

Allen & Unwin New Zealand Pty Ltd with Port Nicholson Press
Compusales Building,
75 Ghuznee Street,
Wellington, New Zealand

British Library Cataloguing in Publication Data

Mitchell, Austin, *1934-*
    Competitive socialism – (The Fabian series)
1. Great Britain. Political parties: Labour Party
(Great Britain). Economic policies
I. Title II. Series
330.941′0858
ISBN 0–04–440431–X

Typeset in 10 on 11 point Garamond by
Input Typesetting Ltd, London SW19 8DR
and printed in Great Britain by
Cox & Wyman, Reading

Contents

General Editor's Preface

The purpose of the Fabian Research Unit series of short books, written by leading experts, is to help develop a new radicalism based on principles of equality, fairness and collective responsibility. The studies are aimed at politicians, civil servants, policy specialists, journalists, party activists and – especially – members of the socially concerned public. They are 'Fabian' in their focus on the political and administrative means of achieving goals. They take no refuge in cautious moderation, but seek instead a rational extremism, exploring the limits of possible progress.

If you are trying to work out a genuinely radical programme, you have difficulties in the face of a right-wing government that is actually carrying through drastic reforms of its own. The biggest difficulty, of course, is the air of unreality that surrounds any proposal until there is the prospect of a transfer of power. At the same time, there is the frustration of trying to shoot at a moving target.

Should you stick doggedly to the substance of old policies, regardless of circumstances? Should you promise to undo most of what has been done during the last ten years? Or should you accept the new measures as a *fait accompli*, however much you may have opposed them when they were introduced? One reason why an affirmative answer to any of these questions is so unpalatable is that it concedes the initiative to the government, and makes the alternative seem either old-fashioned or negative or defeatist.

Yet there is another option. You can observe that the world has indeed moved on and that the problems facing the nation have changed. You can conclude that the action required of a future administration has altered accordingly and that a new programme will have to be more imaginative, not less. You can frankly acknowledge, without concession, that if the Right has broken some of the taboos against innovation, that at least is to be welcomed. And you can look at every issue with a fresh mind, in the search for a serious originality.

Unfortunately, it is easier to call for new ideas than to have them. There exists no philosopher's stone, awaiting its alchemist;

advance is more likely to come through hard work than sudden inspiration. Nevertheless there is already a ferment of discussion on policy, as this series will show.

Each book is a personal contribution and does not necessarily reflect the view of the Unit, or of the Fabian Society with which it is associated. Every topic is approached in a different way. Some authors, for example, are more definite in their prescriptions than others. What they have in common is a concern for the future and an impatience with stale arguments inherited from the past. They share a belief that the vogue for reactionary and neo-liberal panaceas cannot be met either by reviving old remedies or by meekly travelling some distance down the Thatcherite road. They also share a belief that it is pointless to offer a solution without analysing the problem first.

What they intend to do is to expose the failure of existing and former policy, including – where appropriate – policy under earlier administrations; to undermine the convenient theory that a requirement of economic efficiency is inequality and social neglect; and, above all, to consider how, in the world as it has become, real needs can be met.

Ben Pimlott

Preface and Acknowledgements

We socialists are so inhibited by the daring, revolutionary nature of our evangel that when it comes to economics – the only weapon by which the better society can be built – we become cautious, coy and conformist, and fail as a result. Ten years in the frustration of opposition, and one year of shadow responsibility for smokestack industries, have convinced me that there can be no socialism and no salvation for this crumbling country unless we master money and use it for the purposes of the people, not to screw an ever growing tribute from them. When interest rates are at insane levels in a country awash with money, where resources, and far too many people, are unemployed, something is wrong.

Hopefully this might indicate why. It couldn't have been written without Shaun Stewart. Yet many others, Nick Butler, Bryan Gould, Henry Neuburger, and that most patient of editors, Ben Pimlott, have saved me from myself. Dawne Seaton typed it all and lived to tell the tale and the Grimsby Labour Party glazed over as I tried the ideas out on them. Like my family, they all survived. I'm grateful to all of them.

Austin Mitchell
Grimsby, January 1989

For Kiri

Chapter 1
Goodbye Jerusalem

The story of post-war Britain is one of failure. The economy has failed to compete and grow and though not the world's first undeveloping country yet, Britain is certainly its laggard. The welfare society it supports has failed to keep up with needs and expectations, slipping backwards from altruism, betterment and the steady process of raising standards – which goes with strength and progress – to unacceptable levels of unemployment and poverty and a mean shoddiness that have all the hallmarks of a poor society. The political parties, too, have failed: Labour to fulfil the expectations it rouses, relegated to one-shot governments and now completely exiled from power; the Conservatives to succeed in each of their recent incarnations – noblesse oblige under Macmillan, and boom and bust under Ted Heath. Now the jury has just come in on free market fanaticism under Margaret Thatcher, which has come full circle from glacial freeze to another grinding halt in a stop–go cycle she claimed to have banished. A sad saga. It is almost a reverse miracle for a nation which started out well ahead, and a futile failure in a world characterised, otherwise, by success stories.

Blame becomes a litany. Labour blames itself for not being socialist enough. Mrs Thatcher blames the nation, its workers and its past, for not living up to her. The media make a living out of exacerbating our national masochism. Yet the root cause of the failure is economic. The British economy has fallen behind, much of the time comparatively, at times absolutely. Britain came out of the war with a powerful economy largely intact, producing at full power – still one of the workshops of the world – generating a quarter of its trade in manufactured goods – sustaining full employment, a high standard of living, a pioneer welfare state. From there it was downhill all the way, until now we are left with only 7 per cent of world trade, imports of manufactured goods and round half our own sales going to the domestic market. We can neither pay our way in the world nor provide jobs for, or even fulfil the straitened aspirations of, our people. The standard of living is down to eighteenth in twenty-four OECD countries. Even that has been supported only by the accidental blessing of North Sea oil, much of which is now gone.

The consequences are horrendous as comparative decline, now resumed, turns inevitably into absolute decline. Repairing the damage and making up the lost ground are intimidating tasks. The Thatcher government attempted neither, shifting things round vigorously, changing little. The next government must rebuild, for gradually falling behind is a luxury in the face of the hard prospects which lie ahead. The oil contribution will run down in the nineties and we will be net importers after 1991. The blessing of North Sea oil which we have used only as a prop will be kicked away. The imports we have become addicted to, buying abroad what we can no longer make here, are already impossible on the scale we crave them. Industry is too small for us to pay our way in the world and provide jobs for our people, yet is screwed down to its contracted level by high interest rates to depress demand and the power of the competition. Unless it is allowed to grow, massively, to re-create millions of the jobs it has lost, and reverse in less than a decade the failures of four, absolute decline follows and everything turns sour. The British economy ceases to be viable, the first industrial nation becomes the first to go and we slump into becoming a pathetic periphery to Europe. Not because we want to, but because we have no strength to resist the compounding processes of decline. The class and interest competition for shares will become cut throat as the cake shrinks. The subclass will grow ever bigger. Politicians who have proclaimed so endlessly that the British are at their best with their 'backs to the wall' will have the chance to assess the accuracy of their claim, though fascism, despair and desperation are more likely reactions than united endeavour. Socialism and altruism die in cold climates – so can nations which export people, capital, brains, skills, becoming merely industrial backwaters.

The Tories will not make ready for a disaster they don't even see. They have begun to believe their own propaganda, and can't in any case, admit that the years of high oil revenues and low prosperity have been used to rearrange deck chairs on the *Titanic* and improve life on the first-class decks as the ship sinks lower. In difficulties they will turn to batons rather than the bribes and blarney currently used to keep the lower decks happy. Their hallowed market is little use when it turns sour. Yet they have no alternative, being incapable of using the state or cooperating with the people.

Labour can do the job – provided it develops the policies. It is the party of the nation; its task has been saving that nation from the consequences of Tory folly, so it is eager to take up the task. Yet is it competent? Labour is a party of ideology, not economics; conformist and orthodox rather than daring; better at spending than production; cushioning failure rather than building success. Even now it is busily developing policies to rebuild the welfare state and the health service, expand education, generate employment from central and local government, but cannot as yet cope with the basic problem of an economy which can no longer compete.

Rebuilding must be Labour's central priority. Everything else depends on it. New plans for the health service are exercises in futility unless the economic problem is solved. Glowing prospects for change will be doomed to disappointment, as they were after 1964, unless we know how to promote growth. We can indict Tory governments with the most devastating critique, but to what effect if we have no workable alternative? Even our current, and necessary, shift to market socialism is irrelevant unless we solve the problems of production and competitiveness. We require the policies to deliver 3 million jobs and return to full employment, to rebuild our industrial base, to set the economy going and growing at full power, to win back the ground lost and embark on the self-sustaining growth competitors have enjoyed. For all that we must understand the economy and its real dynamics.

Socialists can't defy gravity. Unemployment, lack of competitiveness, slow growth are not weaknesses of capitalism which can be exorcised by socialism. Nor can we legislate a balance of payments surplus or merely require competitiveness. Arguments about who owns an uncompetitive economy are irrelevant, though public ownership can extend as industry collapses into the arms of the state. All too many of our staple reflexes are not socialist but responses to decline. Real socialism is an enlarging prospect. It depends on the powerful heartbeat of a healthy economy. As that faltered we turned, in the past, to substitutes: financing spending out of taxation and borrowing, not production; attempting redistribution of a cake which was not growing fast enough to make the business painless or to benefit the mass of people who looked to us; saving industry by nationalisation when we could not build it by competent economic management; dealing with inflation by means of an incomes policy because we couldn't expand production. All these are artificial substitutes for the proper understanding of a modern industrial economy and how it works.

We have all too little idea how to exercise and expand the industrial heart and set it working properly to pump out the rich oxygenated blood of growth. In that sense West Germany and Japan are more socialist than us, for real socialism is ends – the better society, what we do with the wealth we generate – not means, be they public ownership, planning, redistribution, or even reselection. Our mission is not to eliminate capitalism and capitalists, finance and financiers. It is to make them work better, more efficiently, and for the people. We will be considered competent by the British people only when we know that, and master the task. We must be considered competent if we are to win power. People need confidence in a party. They must think it able to do the job it pretends to.

Socialism is not about making everyone white collar and middle class like Labour MPs. Nor is the better society built by removing people from the coal face, the furnace, the lathe, the shop floor, the world they know, even if it's strange to our articulate spokesmen. Prising people loose from what they have done and are trained to do, but providing no alternative, is ruin, not redemption. The better society rests on a base of jobs, skills, production and survival in the world, not ideas, and the world our people want is a better version of the one they knew, or in lucky cases, still work in. Advancement for them comes, as it always has, through industry, skills, high pay, the platform of a job to stand on to face the world. As it lost sight of that, Labour lost its role. A Labour analysis starts from the point of view of industry, jobs, work, production and making the cake bigger.

At the last election we offered a bit of state and a lot of heart. Neither was enough. Government seemed competent, Labour spendthrift, things were picking up, change looked risky. The last two circumstances will have changed by 1991. Our task is to change the first two. Promising fairer shares of decline, protection for our friends, cuts in consumption as if it was evil, more public spending we can't pay for, or higher taxation to pay for better services are poor substitutes for competence, confidence and the sense of purpose which springs from real understanding and the knowledge that we have the answers. The prospects for success are greater than ever before. The scale of the damage wilfully done to the real economy by Tory incompetence and irresponsibility is the measure of our opportunity. To grasp it we need a proper sense of priorities, an understanding that our central task is to revive 3 million jobs and that those must mainly come from industrial regeneration, the competence to rebuild the economy and the policies to bring all that about. All these come neither from existing doctrines and ideology nor from our previous experience. On growth, jobs, industrial competitiveness, real dynamics our record has been inadequate since 1951. We must go back to study what has gone wrong with the British economy, to begin to understand how to put it right.

Chapter 2
The Exchange Rate as Villain

In Britain, economics is treated as a branch of morality; not so much a guide to running a healthy economy as an opportunity to mobilise and dole out the blame for the failure to do so. To ask what went wrong is to unleash both a chorus of blame and a list of candidates to hang it on. Each element of a class-divided society blames the other. Workers blame management and vice versa. Class blames class, Labour blames Tory and Democrats both, for political parties have become conspiracies to apportion blame. Mrs Thatcher blames everyone, except herself.

More rational explanations also abound. We have paid ourselves more than we produce. We invest too little: productivity and commitment are low: management is bad, the unions worse. The decline of the industrial spirit means that industry does not attract the right ability: the élite go into arts, administration, the media, professions, property, anything but the messy business of making things. We are complacent, lethargic, averse to risk. We think small; manufacturers look for niches, workers for cosy numbers or early redundancy and retirement. Divisions of class are carried over into the industrial battle between shopfloor and management, unions and employers, finance and industry, all preoccupied with status and each other rather than the collective effort of the company, the industry or the country. Political changes, more numerous here than in most of our competitors, mean major changes of policy. The list of explanations is endless.

All these have two characteristics in common. No one provides the single, all embracing cause for a failure as comprehensive as Britain's; some contradict others, everyone mixes their own cocktail. They are also, without exception, consequences rather than causes. A society which has failed hardens in all the characteristics inimical to success. These are they. Divisions widen because group fights group for shares instead of succeeding together. Unions are defensive, workers take industrial action to get what growth doesn't provide. Firms polarise because there is no success to unite them.

Industry doesn't attract because it fails. Governments are thrown out because they don't deliver. Nothing succeeds like success – or frustrates like failure. A Britain which had grown would have been a Britain transformed.

British experience, compared to competitors, points to the pattern. Other economies were run for growth. We were not. They had to build, or rebuild, their peoples were prepared to accept sacrifices and stringencies as a result. We did not, and relaxed, rewarding a tired nation with welfare and affluence. They got on an automatic escalator. We coasted, woke up belatedly, then cast around desperately for answers. Their policies paid and they stuck to the formula, compounding success. We got worse without noticing because we were also getting better than we had been, though ever further behind them in output, productivity, investment and growth. We did not grow because we did not grow. What triggered the divergence and widened the gap?

Germany, Japan, Italy, France and the other, later industrialising countries started with a *tabula* more or less *rasa*, plus undervalued currencies. The first provided the need, the second the opportunity. Exporting paid because of the exchange rate. This attracted investment to exporting industries, so productivity grew. Exports became even more competitive and productivity increased even more with production, a concept so simple it is appreciated everywhere but in Britain, where productivity is seen as a measure of the work ethic. Their home markets were poor, relatively inefficient, and consequently less welcoming to imports than Britain's. As they built up, their internationally traded sectors diverged from the home economy, becoming insulated from its inefficiencies and inflation. They looked to export-led growth, not the domestic consumer, and brought down export prices because of productivity-based economies of scale. Their domestic industry was much less efficient, but with exports scale brought the ability to spread the costs of better research, design, investment, quality control, model changes, and every other 'non-price' factor over a larger output. Growth and the economy were export led. Success snowballed in a process of continuous, cumulative improvement which fed on itself.

We sank, never glimpsing the virtuous cycle, even when Mrs Thatcher made virtue government policy. In a competitive world those who miss out on cumulative improvement face cumulative decline. Growth was not a paramount priority. Our powerful financial sector was more interested in money than production and loomed much larger, so that the destabilising effect of financial fluctuations and the burdens of fulfilling financial goals such as high interest rates, 'sound' money, or 'countering inflation' bore heavily on our industry. Where industry looked in, finance looked out to the sterling area, the Eurodollar market, the EEC, the world. For industry it was alien and unhelpful, rather than supportive and subordinate as it was elsewhere. Our domestic market was more profitable, behind its tariff, than unprofitable exports. We started with an overvalued currency, so exporting never really paid, and certainly did not generate the profits for reinvestment that it was providing for our competition. Exports were surplus production; what could be spared from the home market, not industry's whole existence. So growth was consumption-led, governed by the state of demand at home, not exports. British industry grew more slowly and was consistently less profitable than its competitors. Hence it invested less and improved less, so its products became less attractive; lower value, higher cost. The return on exports did not make it worthwhile to build extra capacity, so the growth of exports followed the slow growth of productive capacity rather than lead it. We were reluctant exporters. Our internationally traded sector never grew enough to free itself from the home market with its inflationary pressures or to achieve the economies of scale and the productivity of competitors. Growth did not upset our settled ways, stimulate innovation, or generate that restless thirst for change which is the hallmark of the competitive economy. It was led by domestic demand, and that progressed only slowly as living standards rose. Caution paid; risk did not.

Others grew. We had stop–go. Each acceleration produced bottle-necks in production, skills, capacity, supplies, all generating inflation. Imports were sucked in, more each time, going up on a ratchet, threatening the balance of payments and endangering the exchange rate. So each time expansion built up, government damped demand by ever higher interest rates, greater restrictions on credit, tougher controls on prices and incomes, and ever harsher taxation and deflation. Other nations grew continuously by boosting industry. We disciplined it. As go turned to stop anyone who had taken risks by investing or expanding was penalised by higher interest rates and reduced demand. Caution became a conditioned reflex. Defensive driving makes sense in the slow lane.

The effects are made dramatically clear by the experience of one crucial industry: motor cars; central to the manufacturing sector, crucial to manufacturing skills and processes, vital to the regional economy, and Scotland, to jobs and to the balance of payments – in 1986 our deficit on trade in cars was half the deficit on all manufactured trade. This industry is therefore fundamental to economic health; and archetypal in its illustration of what went wrong.

The petrol engine was pioneered by the Germans. The French developed it, remaining the largest producer until the late 1920s. The small UK industry got its chance after 1931 when Britain devalued by going off the gold standard while France didn't. By 1937 the booming British industry was producing 114 per cent more cars than in 1929 and exporting 133 per cent more. France's output was 12 per cent lower. The £100 car arrived, Britain got cumulative advantages it had experienced before only in cotton.

The post-war story was the reverse. Things started well. World-wide shortages and suppressed demand created a sellers' market and Britain exported nearly 80 per cent of its production. Yet production was the problem. The industry had to pound out the product from existing, old factories. It never rebuilt to economies of scale by concentrating on big modern plants on industrially convenient green field sites. It had too many marques from too many plants. Instead of producing everything 'in house' it relied on components from outside suppliers, an advantage in the 1930s when it allowed economies of scale not then available to any car manufacturer except Ford at Dagenham, but leading to lack of control of stocks, output and quality when it began to face competition from giants on the world stage.

Regional policy spread plants to Merseyside and Scotland away from the national centre of production, the West Midlands, further reducing the effectiveness of management and adding transport and distribution costs. Economies of scale are crucial in the volume car industry. VW, Renault, Fiat grew to them quickly with output soon running to millions and coming from a few huge plants. We struggled along in the best British tradition of make do and mend. Economies of scale eluded us; production difficulties and bottlenecks in overstretched, scattered plants dogged us; the industry never invested on any adequate scale. It simply fell behind, dogged by high prices and a bad reputation for poor back-up service and quality which became a weakness as markets became increasingly competitive and choosy.

Exports stagnated in the sixties, fell in the seventies. The industry became ever more reliant on its home market. That lurched unpredictably rather than grew steadily because of its use as a regulator and because government opted for an August start for the registration year, guaranteeing a demand peak that month which the

Table 1 Car Production (thousands)

Year	United Kingdom	UK Exports	France	Western Germany	Japan	USA
1929	182	24	212	96		4,453
1937	390	54	177	269		3,929
1948	335	224	100	30		3,909
1950	523	398	257	219	2	6,666
1960	1,353	570	1,175	1,817	165	6,675
1970	1,641	690	2,458	3,528	3,179	6,550
1975	1,268	516	2,546	2,908	4,568	6,717
1980	924	359	2,939	3,521	7,038	6,376
1981	955	156	2,612	3,578	6,974	6,253
1982	868	313	2,777	3,761	6,882	5,073
1983	1,045	274	2,961	3,878	7,152	6,781
1984	909	219	2,713	3,790	7,073	7,773
1985	1,048	240	2,632	4,167	7,647	8,185
1986	1,019	201	2,773	4,311	7,810	7,829
1987	1,143	245	3,051	4,371	7,891	7,098
1988	1,226		3,223	4,346	8,198	7,110

British industry, striving to keep going by string and elastic-band production methods, could not possibly meet.

Demand rose and fell because hire-purchase restrictions, interest rates and demand management were the government's only weapons to tackle balance of payments problems. Expansion produced peaks like the Barber boom pushing home sales up to an all-time high of 1,294,000, straining the industry. Stops produced troughs like the Selwyn Lloyd squeeze of 1961 reducing sales to 633,000 and domestic output by 26 per cent. Every other industry grew steadily and in the seventies the gap compounded when, with the car industry's enthusiastic support, Britain joined the Common Market. The home market itself became vulnerable, with the loss of an 11 per cent tariff on imports from the EEC and of a valuable tariff advantage in the Commonwealth, the European Free Trade Association, and the Irish Republic. Exports fell every year until output is now only double the levels of the early fifties.

It was hardly the design or engineering of the cars. The Morris Minor was a brilliant innovation and better than most competitors. It was never continuously updated and improved within the old shell as was the VW Beetle. The Hillman and the Standard Vanguard were better than most competitors as were the Triumph Herald, the Rover 2000, the Triumph 2000. The Mini was a brilliant innovation but too expensive to produce at a competitive price without making a loss on each one sold. The Land and Range

Rovers were equally brilliant but far too expensive to exploit their potential. All were well engineered, poorly produced, for neither investment nor the scale of production reached the levels necessary to sustain quality control, bring unit costs down and use the classic techniques of pricing to markets to win them. Keeping production going in difficult circumstances was enough strain on British management.

Price is crucial in mass consumer markets. The so-called 'non-price' factors depend on it because they require profits to produce the investment to allow improvement in research, design, development and quality control. Scale of production spreads those costs over a large and increasing output, adding less of each to each unit cost. Good management and design have to be paid for, good workmanship depends on keeping good labour from moving elsewhere. Meeting delivery dates means holding stocks or changing production schedules to meet the order. Quality means paying for inspection and control. All improvements in performance cost money and that must be recovered in the price of the product.

An initial advantage on price through the exchange rate is therefore used to graduate quickly to the cumulative benefits of scale. This institutionalises and amplifies the price advantages, adds the non-price ones to it. Thus the VW Beetle, an outdated design and a clumsy car, sold because it was cheap through the very low German exchange rate of the late forties and early fifties. Exporting was profitable, indeed essential for a country desperate to earn foreign exchange to build up its industry, and the profits were invested to upgrade the product and win reputations for service and reliability. The Renault Dauphine had a dashing image but was unreliable. It was, however, cheap and the French industry doubled production in four years after the double devaluations in 1957–8. Japanese cars were rust tubs, stodgy and underengineered, but undervaluation of the yen allowed this industry to increase output elevenfold in ten years.

Profits mean investment, means improvement, means economies of scale, mean more new models, mean better cars and quality control, mean even bigger sales, mean ability to price to markets and build them by advertising and efficient networks. Competitors gained on every count; we lost. They doubled, trebled, quadrupled, output and concentrated it in fewer and newer plants. The German industry overtook ours by 1956, the French by 1964, the Japanese by 1968, the Italians by 1975, then the Spanish. Collectively, EEC producers, with nearly 40 per cent, almost overtook us in our own home market. By 1973, West Germany produced twice as many cars as us in far fewer plants, exporting two-thirds of its output compared to only half in the fifties. France had increased its share of exports from a third to a half over the same period. These exports were crucial to scale.

By contrast, the British industry languished. Our exchange rate was high for most of the time, so profits were low, exports marginal. Production remained small scale and inefficient. The industry became increasingly vulnerable and now the only domestic producer, Rover, gets the worst of all worlds: too small, at an output of just over 400,000, to be a volume producer; not sufficiently invested in to be a specialist; sinking slowly between the stools.

The exchange rate is the hidden hand shaping these destinies. It has boosted our competition and defeated us. Even in America, the giant of the world car industry, overvaluation of the dollar reduced US output by 1982 to 5,073,000, slightly below the 5,119,000 cars produced in 1948, a mere 10 per cent above the 1929 figure. In each case observers see a production system which is failing, as in Britain, or succeeding as in Germany or Japan and condemn, or praise, accordingly, blaming strikes, bad workmanship, bad design, low quality or even national characteristics of laziness or strike proneness; praising hard work, technical competence and training, better management and labour relations. None is the initial cause, all are symptoms developing because higher or lower prices held back or boosted. The industry is basically simple but diverged rapidly as failure or success worked their magic. The currency was the trigger, the sustaining cause, the hidden hand giving one industry a running start, imposing a ball and chain on ours, precipitating the cumulative processes which then came into play on both.

Manufacturing caters for mass markets where price is crucial. Britain's post-war failure is a compound of many similar experiences in different industries. Competitiveness and uncompetitiveness are both self-sustaining. Cumulative improvement ensues from an undervalued exchange rate. Cumulative deterioration ensures that costs rise with an overvalued exchange rate so markets are given up. Economies of scale in internationally traded goods are much greater than in other industries, as they must be to overcome the higher cost of transport, selling abroad and setting up of distribution networks. Hence the benefits of exports and growth are disproportionate and quickly generate a virtuous cycle through falling costs, or in decline cause the vicious circle of import-led contraction and rising costs. Costs and prices in export industries rise, or fall, faster than costs and prices generally.

International trade arises not because some economies are more efficient than others, or some people harder working, but because each produces some things more efficiently than others. With exchange rates correctly aligned each country specialises in the goods it is relatively good at producing, even though everything could be produced more efficiently elsewhere. Exchange rate equilibrium ensures that it remains competitive in those goods and that there is no general shift of economic activity to more efficient economies.

Comparative advantage is not inevitable as Lancashire's natural one in cotton is supposed to have come from a damp climate. Rather than an endowment of capital, labour, or resources, or national intelligence, it can be created. The instrument is the exchange rate. On the back of competitiveness compounded by cumulative processes, the sustaining network of skills and training, the research endowment, the networks of suppliers and services, the complex, interdependent systems of an industrial economy are built up. It can also be lost by the exchange rate, as industries become uncompetitive and networks of suppliers, producers, training, skills disintegrate so the sustaining web frays. Industrialising countries realised that comparative advantage is no inevitable law and deliberately set out to build it, coming, as in the Japanese car industry, from nowhere on the basis of careful calculation about which markets to enter, which industries to build. Having inherited our advantage we assumed it was God-given and threw it away.

As a market-clearing mechanism the exchange rate is competitive if it enables a country to balance its overseas accounts in conditions of full employment, and preferably at a high and sustainable rate of growth. An individual industry is competitive if the rate of return on export sales is at least as high as on domestic ones, and high enough to justify investment in new capacity. That means, unless the industry has special funding, a return at least as high as those of overseas competitors. Few industries in Britain have met these requirements at any time since the war, and not too many in the US either, though that matters less with their bigger home market. British industry generally has been consistently less profitable than its competitors but it coasted along on advantages and investments inherited from the nineteenth century, or the great reinvestment of the war and the thirties and hardly sought to sustain either.

The early success of the Germans and Japanese cannot be attributed to hard work, higher productivity, higher technology or superior goods. Output per head in German manufacturing was lower than that of the UK. German and Japanese products were cheaper because of the exchange rate. Never having that platform to build on, our industry became progressively more exposed instead of succeeding. Labour-intensive industries like textiles were the first to go because the exchange rate made our labour costs high compared to competitors. Firms with the highest costs in each industry led the way. None of them died for want of trying. They went because the exchange rate moved their goal posts. In an increasingly competitive world manufacturing must get on or get out, grow or decline. Ours didn't grow and became vulnerable. Industries lost market share overseas then faced challenge on the home market. The cumulative process was described as early as 1887 by the Minority Report of the *Royal Commission on the Depression of Trade and Industry*:

> any industry in a hopeless struggle against insoluble difficulties must sooner or later fall into a condition of languor, and of decreasing ability to meet competition. Those in it lose heart and hope: capital and talent are gradually withdrawn from it; and as it offers reduced remuneration and diminished prospect of advancement to skilled labour, the quality of labour employed in it tends continually to decline and its production deteriorates.

It is a vivid forecast of what happened to textiles, to motor bikes, to cars, to British manufacturing in general, omitting only the industrial relations problems failure generates.

Those industries need not have died. There is a rate of exchange to fit every industrial structure. If an overvalued currency makes it appear that there is no demand for outdated resources made idle, that is because the rate is too high. Resources will move from low-wage to high-wage industries when the rate is competitive. There is a rate of exchange which ensures that every economy can make full use of its resources and one which ensures it cannot, however efficient, however well invested. The first is the rate of exchange Britain has had so rarely, and then only for brief, transient periods.

Chapter 3
Sterling Follies, 1945–88

The exchange rate is crucially important to an industrial economy and Britain's post-war history is the long, sad saga of the way it has been mishandled. The failure is so great that it cannot be put down to simple incompetence but rather to something with even deeper roots in our psyche and society. British attitudes to the exchange rate are unique. Competitors were realistic because battered economies and their desperate need for overseas exchange made exchange rates low. Having seen the value of competitive exchange rates, governments to whom industry was central as the instrument of reconstruction and nation-building kept them down by every available means: exchange control on foreign capital imports, negative interest rates on incoming money, keeping interest rates low or, later, exporting capital. Some rise was inevitable as industries became ever more competitive and the balance of payments turned from deficit to enormous surplus which could not be absorbed in the reserves. Anything substantial was strenuously resisted.

In Britain, the exchange rate was not an instrument but an aspect of morality, 'sterling virtue', a legacy of empire with a worldwide role, even a symbol of the nation; and sometimes a phallic one with Britain proud when it was hard, reduced to post-imperial triste when not. The media see it as a national fever chart, a convenient measure of performance. As it shrinks, so does the nation, for the chattering classes chatter to the middle class, a fifth column of internationalists seeing a strong pound as the support for their own cosmopolitanism from foreign cars to Perrier water. The public were all too easily taken in. In a consumer society, a high exchange rate buys more, and the best developed consumer market in Europe inevitably saw benefits in a high exchange rate in cheap imports and cheap holidays. The effects on output and employment, and the burdens and costs these impose on the consumer as taxpayer were the inevitable consequences, but they emerged only in the long term.

A government with heavy overseas commitments and an imperial mentality liked the high exchange rate which made both easier to bear. Britain, with its commitments east of Suez, its strong presence in Germany, and the colonial empire, had the largest overseas presence of any competitor, except the USA, while the sterling area forced a commitment to sustain the exchange rate as the trustee of reserves in London. As the sterling area faded away, new political considerations intervened. As the British economy failed to grow governments could satisfy electorates by keeping the exchange rate high to buy what exports couldn't. They used the same weapon to fight inflation, the consequence of failure, and to buy more while producing less, again to please electorates.

Competitors depended on industry, the sector with the strongest interest in a low exchange rate. Our industry was less important, less well organised, more taken for granted and hardly vociferous or perceptive about its real interests. Its attitudes were complacent and defensive, it went for niches and safety rather than expansion and risks. Finance had grown strong on the back of a huge mercantile empire. It had an importance paralleled in few other countries. Proud, and centred in the City, close to government's ear (where in every competing economy it was weaker and removed geographically from government) finance, embracing the Bank of England, Lloyds, the banks, insurance companies, the stock market and the worldwide money manipulators of the City, saw its own as the national interest, the pound as its instrument. This required certainty in the exchange rate and an overvalued currency buys more investments overseas than a competitive one. Banks too prefer high interest rates, the prop underpinning a high exchange rate. They pay their customers little or nothing on current accounts, so 'the spread', the gap between the cost of funds and the rate of interest they receive, widens as rates go up. They now raise more of their capital in the market and pay going rates, but still prefer high to low rates because banks, unlike building societies, create credit out of their deposits, multiplying the sums they receive. Other banking systems, investing more in industry, favoured the low interest rates which help it. Ours lend more heavily to property, personal lending, consumption, takeovers, house purchase, all impervious to high rates.

Britain entered the post-war struggle for survival with the attitudes and equipment appropriate to an imperial clipper race. Our competitors, leaner, fitter and more single-minded, trained for the manufacturing marathon. In the age of mass affluence and mass demand this was the right race. Repeating the mistake made after the First World War, we shouldered the cross of the pre-war exchange rate, £1 = $4.20 against the dollar. Competitors got away with very low rates because there was no industrial or trading history to fix them by. For us the rate became a burden, for them an opportunity. On American insistence we accepted the principle of non-discrimination built into the General Agreement on Tariffs and Trade (GATT) which meant phasing out those imperial preferences which had effectively enlarged our home market before the war, as well as the restrictions on imports from the dollar area which protected British industry after it. Keynes's original proposals for Bretton Woods involved symmetry between the obligations of debtors and creditors. They were rejected by allowing creditor countries, which the United States thought they would be indefinitely, to pile up huge surpluses without any changes in policy required. Deficit countries, which we became, were compelled to sacrifice internal growth to external equilibrium by deflating when in difficulties.

The consequences came as the world recovered. Britain's growth was restricted by capacity and supply problems. As Germany's problems of reconstruction and feeding its workers were solved they roared ahead, boosted by a great supply of labour from the East, new factories with the latest machinery laid out in a cost-efficient way which could not be achieved in our multistoreyed mills and scattered engineering plants, and the gap in export markets created by British and American rearmament in the Korean War. Currency relativities had to be adjusted in 1949 to allow a revaluation of the dollar and though the pound came down by 30 per cent, the D-Mark by 20 per cent, the scope for expansion to take advantage of this was far greater in Germany. UK exports rose by 12 per cent between the first nine months of 1949 and the second quarter of 1950, German by 163 per cent. The share of exports in total manufacturing output increased in Germany and in the other industrial countries which devalued. In the UK, exports merely kept pace with output increase. Germany then fed on its initial boost. Its volume of exports doubled again in the year ending September 1951, in Britain they went up by 19 per cent. With 1949 as a hundred, German exports were 412 in 1952, 854 in 1957, British 112 and 137.

Devaluation boosted British industry though much of the boost was diverted to rearmament. In Germany, it precipitated the economic miracle. The huge increase in production and exports brought about a reduction in costs, making exports even more attractive. German export prices fell substantially and even by 1957 their consumer price index had reached only 109 compared to Britain's 147. In 1950, a Board of Trade Memorandum on the first year of devaluation warned that British exports would increase 'at best no faster than either our own increase in output or the expansion of world trade – both limiting our progress to very moderate rates'. In 1952, the Treasury, aware of the same problem, urged convertibility of sterling which would have allowed the exchange rate to adjust. This was vetoed by Churchill. Britain was to stick to fixed exchange rates. So without a powerful internationally traded sector protected from domestic cost increases by economies of scale and the cumulative improvement of the virtuous cycle, those cost increases passed directly into export prices, leading to a steady real appreciation of sterling, averaging around 1 per cent per annum, weakening us in existing markets and providing no competitive incentive to push into new markets or take risks.

High prices squeezed profits. Exports looked less and less worth bothering about. For competitors they were the lifeblood and the cumulative improvement triggered by a competitive currency powered them ahead; Britain lagged: the slow growth economy. The increase in the volume of exports between 1950 and 1959 was 11 per cent for the UK, 454 per cent for West Germany and 274 per cent for Japan. Our share of main manufacturing country exports of manufactures fell from 25 to 17 per cent, Germany's rose from 7 to 19 per cent. The Japanese, who had doubled theirs from 3.4 to 6.7 per cent, were poised to begin their home run. All these were cumulative processes. Under Bretton Woods there was no way of stopping the momentum, once under way.

Tasting the joys of affluence, becoming better off, we failed to notice the omens. We were growing, but not fast enough to compete. Exports were increasing, but not moving into new markets, and the profit return was too inadequate to encourage firms to boost them or to pay for investment to build them. Cotton, where price is absolutely crucial, best illustrates the process. Output of cotton yarn fell from 416,000 tonnes in 1949 to 275,000 in 1959, though Germany's nearly doubled and Japan's trebled. Other industries just grew too slowly. Few were concerned. Falling food and raw material prices concealed our loss of competitiveness. The huge expansion in world trade disguised its consequences. We floated up with that, but the boat was leaking.

By the late fifties and early sixties critics such as Andrew Schonfield, Michael Shanks (*The Stagnant Society*) and Samuel Brittan were warning of the problems. Perplexed dissatisfaction was growing. Yet refusal to admit that sterling was overvalued confused cause and effect. Everything was blamed but the rate. Other countries used industry to drive their economies. We disciplined it to regulate ours. Domestic demand sustained British industry in the absence of export-led growth, but when it was boosted balance of payments difficulties developed because we had not expanded capacity. So, governments deflated, penalising risk-takers and anyone who had invested to increase production. High interest rates were both the instinctive response to problems and an indispensable prop to a pound whose value had ceased to represent the competitive strength of the British economy, further penalising an industry starved of profits. Britain was trapped by the overvalued exchange rate. Few knew it. Most of those who did would or could not say. Political parties preferred to ignore the issue. Labour, whose promises of growth and expansion were impossible without devaluation, studiously said nothing in opposition and in power, after 1964, defended the exchange rate. Sir Donald Macdougall, Director General of the New Department of Economic Affairs, summed up the reasons given by the party's top men in his book *Don and Mandarin* (1988). In doing so he listed all the prevailing fallacies about a devaluation which he and a few others saw as an escape from Britain's trap. Wilson opposed it

> because he was aware of the economic and political risks that were undoubtedly involved, but also because Balogh [his economic adviser] had persuaded him that it was unnecessary since 'socialist' policies could cure the balance of payments problems in quite a short time: Callaghan, as he told me . . . because he had promised the US Secretary of the Treasury he wouldn't devalue. George Brown because he regarded it as an act against the working class.

Brown changed his mind. The others did not, Labour broke itself in an impossible struggle to defend the indefensible.

Instead of devaluation Labour opted for heavy borrowing and an import surcharge which did nothing to help exports. Foreign borrowing suited the lenders but for us was a costly means of delaying the inevitable, and one which didn't even work. By 1967 exports fell, imports started to rise, Britain went back into the red and Labour was forced to devalue by 14.3 per cent from $2.80 to $2.40. We needed a bigger devaluation to get our prices down to a competitive level and increase profit margins, but 14.3 per cent was the most that the major industrial countries would agree to as part of a package which included credits of $2.9bn and $1.4bn from the IMF, on condition that the UK pursued deflationary fiscal and monetary policies.

The rot stopped. Exports of manufactures rose 14 per cent in volume in 1968 and by a further 13 per cent in 1969, compared to 22 per cent for the whole of the seven years preceding the devaluation. Our share of MMC exports of manufactures rose by 0.2 per cent, the first increase since 1949, and the 1968 balance of payments deficit of £264m moved into a surplus of £484m in 1969, £795m in 1970 and £1,090m in 1971. Credit is usually given to Roy Jenkins' deflation but that was harmful, depressing demand and preventing industry from growing. Manufacturing output rose by 7.6 per cent in 1968 and 3.7 per cent in 1969 but then fell by 0.4 per cent in 1970 and 1.1 per cent in 1971, pushing up wage costs per unit of output and throwing away some of the benefits of devaluation – as well as the life of the Labour government.

Devaluation indicated a slow learning process about the importance of the exchange rate and a realisation of the importance of export-led growth. Unfortunately, the wrong conclusions were drawn. Politicians looked to achieve export success not by the competitive currency competitors had used but by access to the larger market of the European Economic Community. This was, somehow, supposed to effect the miracle on its own. It couldn't because Britain's problem was to expand production, bring down unit costs and get on to a virtuous cycle. EEC membership actually threatened production. British goods could only sell in the wider market if they were competitive against rivals who had already turned economies of scale into cumulative improvement and built a strong position to clobber our more stagnant industries. A section of our existing export trade was threatened by the loss of preference in markets which were both larger than the EEC and better suited to our products. Our home market, because we took down a bigger barrier against them than they against us, became vulnerable. Being bigger and more powerful they could price to win that market.

So the sixties had been the decade when our exports flagged as a result of loss of competitiveness. The seventies became the decade when we lost our home market, for the same reason, compounded now and in the eighties by the EEC.

Intensifying competition in an open market where preferences for British industry were being removed meant that price, and the exchange rate, changed from influential to crucial. Yet in the Smithsonian agreement of December 1971, we misguidedly agreed to let the nominal rate for sterling rise to an average of $2.60 in the first half of 1972. This pushed the non-oil balance of trade well into the red, the most disastrous possible preparation for EEC entry. Britain needed devaluation to survive in the open market. It finally got it when the Heath government allowed sterling to float in June 1972. It sank. From the second quarter of 1972 to the fourth quarter of 1973 the exchange rate fell 9 per cent against the dollar to $2.38 and 27 per cent against the D-Mark to DM 6.06. Coupled with an expansion of credit and the money supply, Britain had belatedly hit on the formula for expansion others had enjoyed for decades. GDP rose by 7.2 per cent in 1973, the fastest increase since the war; so was the rise in manufacturing output by 9.3 per cent. Unemployment fell from 827,000 in the first quarter of 1972 to 462,000 in the fourth quarter of 1973. Britain enjoyed the benefits of a more competitive currency coupled with domestic expansion and British industry responded vigorously. Manufacturing output reached a peak not seen for another fifteen years.

Before this could boost the economy into the virtuous cycle, the expansion was nipped in the bud. A huge increase in world prices for oil, food, and basic raw materials coupled, internally, with a rapid escalation of share, house and asset prices, triggered by the irresponsible abolition of restrictions on bank lending under pressure from the Bank of England, caused inflation to rocket. The expansion was stopped. The learning process ended by reinforcing all the wrong lessons. The Conservative Party rejected Heath and expansion and turned to a glacial monetarism. The Labour government came in not to expand, as socialism requires, but to damp down. Inflation became public enemy number one and deflation an orthodoxy. The only way to fight inflation is by expansion, lowering interest rates, bringing down unit costs, bursting through to economies of scale. Deflation meant the opposite of all these. Coupled with the effects of entry to the EEC, compounded now by high interest rates, the consequences were disastrous. The seventies were a wasted decade.

The Labour government grappled with the consequences. The money supply was increased by less than was required to sustain growth. In every quarter up to the first quarter of 1976, the nominal exchange rate fell as a consequence by less than the increase in domestic prices. It was high because high interest rates were encouraging the inflow of foreign funds. By the first quarter of 1976 the real exchange rate, measured in terms of relative export unit values, was up by 10.5 per cent. That combination produced a vicious squeeze. Unemployment nearly trebled to 1,287,000 in the first quarter of 1977.

When the pound came down in 1976 Labour used up the foreign exchange reserves to stop the inevitable, then panicked and turned to the IMF. In Tory mythology, that body taught Labour a lesson.

In fact, it saw that sterling had been overvalued and wanted a monetary and exchange policy consistent with balance of payments equilibrium. To this end, the IMF *Letter of Intent* included a government undertaking that 'stability in exchange markets would be maintained consistently with the continued maintenance of the competitive position of UK manufacturers at home and abroad'.

A monetary target would not have allowed opportunities for the import-saving and export-led growth which that exchange rate offered. So manufacturing targets were set in terms of domestic credit expansion not, as the Bank wanted, in terms of sterling M3. The permitted margin was generous. It was not the IMF but the Bank of England which wanted deflation. It got it by not reducing interest rates sufficiently, so the inflow of funds forced the government to 'uncap' sterling in the summer of 1977. 'Game, set and match to the Bank,' said *The Sunday Times*. The government lamely went along with this because it did not understand what was really happening and because it was politically useful to let sterling float upwards to bring down the cost of living.

The long-term interests of the economy were thus sacrificed to the short-term needs of political survival. Yet even this did not stop Labour's defeat. The real money supply fell by 7 per cent, having already been reduced by 30 per cent since 1974. The nominal, trade-weighted, real exchange rate rose by 11 per cent between the fourth quarter of 1976 and the second quarter of 1979. The real rate expressed in terms of relative export prices in a common currency rose by 25 per cent. The price of imports of finished manufactures relative to exports fell by 15 per cent. Manufacturing output rose only 0.6 per cent in 1978 then declined by 0.2 per cent to 4 per cent less than in the second half of 1973. Unemployment rose again. Thus in Labour's five-year term the real money supply had fallen by 35 per cent and as a result the real exchange rate had risen by 25 per cent. GDP rose a mere 8 per cent, real personal disposable incomes 7 per cent, and real consumer's expenditure only 3 per cent. Manufacturing output fell by 4 per cent. Unemployment rose 149 per cent. Labour forced the unions to play Brutus and Tory triumph did not bring monetarism to power. It was already there. By setting monetary targets, pursuing 'non-accommodating monetary policies', putting up interest rates to fund the borrowing requirement and uncapping sterling, Labour dragged the Trojan horse into the citadel. As usual, we were better at orthodoxies than the Conservatives.

Tory victory merely made monetarism a proclaimed obsession rather than a covert orthodoxy. It was politically useful because it hurt the unions, disciplined industry, strengthened finance and rewarded the 'haves' with high interest rates. Yet it could not have come into full bloom at a more inappropriate time. The pound was pushed up by becoming a petro-currency as oil prices increased. Oil boosted the balance of payments. Monetarism, coupling high interest rates with domestic deflation, turned rise into a rocket ascent, and overvaluation changed from shackle to agent of destruction. Whether deliberately, to increase unemployment and discipline unions, or accidentally, an unintended by-product of policies which got out of control, is a matter of abnormal psychology. Neither reflects much credit on the government. The effects were equally disastrous. A fifth of British manufacturing capacity was closed, 28 per cent of manufacturing jobs were lost. Britain became a net manufacturing importer for the first time since the Industrial Revolution.

Both political parties had competed to be in power to enjoy the oil, which, it was supposed, would trigger the British economic miracle; an opportunity to invest, to expand, to grow through balance of payments problems and to generate new public spending after the long years of comparative decline. Given appropriate fiscal and exchange rate policies, oil could have done that. In fact, it was thrown away because its advent coincided with monetarism, bringing back the worst of the old orthodoxies rolled into one and centred on an overvalued exchange rate. Here is an illustration. The 80 million tonnes of crude oil consumed in UK refineries in the peak year of 1985 was worth £12.8bn at 1985 prices. Net exports of crude oil and petroleum products were worth another £8.1bn, making a total of £21bn. That saving meant exporting £21bn less of other goods than we would have done without North Sea oil; no problems if extraction of crude oil provided a commensurate number of jobs. In the early years of this century exports of coal had made a much bigger contribution to the balance of payments in relative terms but the diversion of resources from manufacturing was of no great consequence. Coal employed one out of ten in the labour force.

Oil and gas employ no such numbers. They are distinguished from every other product by the combination of God's gift and the oil cartel. The cost of extracting oil from most of the North Sea represents only a small fraction of the selling price. In 1985, incomes from the extraction of oil and gas amounted to only £560m, less than 3 per cent of the industry's contribution to GDP of £18,896m. The windfall profit, including the government take amounting to some £11–12bn in 1985, is a tax on the consumer.

This reduces output and employment by a commensurate figure unless the deflationary effect is neutralised, either by a net export of capital or by pumping sufficient public and/or private credit into the system to compensate for the decline in spending. We do not need oil money to pay for imports so long as we have spare capacity to produce such goods for ourselves. If we have that, we are better using it.

The government take from the North Sea is not a transfer of real resources. So if the 'bloody stuff' remained in the ground, the government could print money instead. Which is what they should be doing if they do not want their take to be used up in paying unemployment benefit to those whose jobs have been destroyed. Oil is of no use so long as the economy is less than fully employed. What it could buy from overseas would be better produced here. The problem is not North Sea oil but the double misfortune of having it in combination with deflating economics, rather than using it to fuel expansion. Oil is wasted unless the exchange rate falls to a level which enables us to earn a balance of payments surplus on current account equal to the revenue from it.

The Tory government has never grasped this truth though it has been forced by calamity to pull back from the worst consequences of its own folly. The pound peaked at a real exchange rate of 105.5 in the first quarter of 1981, 46 per cent up on the fourth quarter of 1976. The Prime Minister's Economic Adviser, Professor Walters, then pointed out that higher interest rates to control the money supply meant more borrowing by companies to pay interest bills, and more money flowing into Britain, both leading to an even higher pound and an expansion of the M3 figures, which the whole exercise was meant to bring down in the first place. The lady turned. Expanded domestic credit and overfunding eased the strain, bringing the pound down by 19 per cent to 85.3 in the first quarter of 1983 and preparing the climate for the 1983 election.

This did not, however, mean any conversion to the virtues of a competitive currency, merely that government had at last seen the disastrous consequences of ludicrous overvaluation, and opted instead for substantial overvaluation. Inflation was still higher than the OECD average. The Chancellor pushed the pound back up to 91.7 in the third quarter of 1983 and 93.3 in the third quarter of 1985. The economy was kept spluttering along by an increase in exports to America – where the dollar overvaluation had eclipsed ours – by a falling savings ratio and by the steady increase in real disposable incomes. Nothing here to restore the damage – yet much better than 1979–81.

Then, in 1986, the oil price fell. A country whose manufacturing had shrunk had a petro-currency and the pound fell from 90.8 in the second quarter of 1986 to 82.9 in the fourth, despite the increases in interest rates to stop it. The fall against the D-Mark between the third quarter of 1985 and February 1987 was over 30 per cent; exactly the devaluation Peter Shore had proposed in November 1982 and which the Chancellor had denounced as wildly irresponsible. The results were as beneficial as Peter Shore predicted. Manufactured exports rose 6 per cent, the rate of inflation did not increase, industry revived. Unit costs rose more slowly than those of stagnant West Germany. Britain was rediscovering *in extremis* what other economies had glimpsed long ago: that growth is good for you.

The government had neither anticipated nor wanted the fall in the exchange rate which stimulated the expansion. It had done all it could to stop it. Now it took the credit for the consequences, used the increased VAT and Corporation Tax to cut income tax, and called an election on the theme of 'some of you have never had it so good', proclaiming that Britain was at last enjoying its own economic miracle of sustained growth and rising productivity. In fact, just as President Reagan had borrowed 3 trillion dollars from the Japanese to throw a party, rather than seizing its opportunity for real growth, Mrs Thatcher was using North Sea oil to throw her own, meaner party. But it was not a miracle, merely a go phase of the old stop–go cycle. After a depression on the scale of 1979–82 the potential for rapid recovery is enormous so British growth was really half cooked: 4.2 per cent in 1987, mainly generated by consumption, quickly deemed unsustainable and not very good compared to 4.5 per cent in 1959, 7.2 per cent in 1973 or 3.2 per cent annual average in the decade to 1973. After nine years, manufacturing output struggled marginally above 1979 levels but was still 4 per cent below those of 1973. Excluding industries like defence or building materials, not exposed to heavy foreign competition, output was 14 per cent below that year. Productivity rose but the 3.3 per cent annual average rate of increase in output per person hour in manufacturing from 1979 to 1987 was lower than the 4.7 per cent in the decade to 1973, and much of it was down to plant closures and the decline of labour intensive industries. Taking the whole labour force, employed and unemployed, there was no increase from 1979 to 1986.

The improvement was pathetic compared to both need and opportunity. Yet it was promptly aborted by the government itself. This was defended as necessary to deal with overheating. Yet an economy in which there are no shortages is one in which there is no incentive for resources to move from less to more productive uses, and a denial of the price system. No economy with 3 million people out of work can be overheated. The problem was the maldistribution of growth, concentrated in the overcrowded, expensive, bottle-necked South-East rather than spread to those parts of the country where resources were underused. Overheating was largely a financial phenomenon of asset inflation. The credit explosion led to an escalation of house and asset prices which then became a justification for more credit in a process of continuous creation of collateral, inflating the North Sea Bubble. That arose from the Chancellor's refusal to control or direct credit. Leaving it to the market meant channelling it to the highest bidder: housing, consumer demand, takeovers and asset speculation. Trying to control this by interest rates was futile because these demands were relatively resistant to rises, though industry, whose investment plans were always vulnerable, was not.

The instrument which Nigel Lawson used to kill the goose which had laid his golden eggs was the exchange rate. Interest rates, already double West Germany's were put up by a third, thus pushing the pound up. The real value of sterling in terms of trade weighted relative export prices rose by 21 per cent between the fourth quarter of 1986 and the second of 1988. That of the D-Mark, the currency whose undervaluation was largely responsible for Europe's problems, fell by 4 per cent.

The consequences of that overvaluation was the balance of payments deficit as imports became cheap, producing a deficit running at 3 per cent, over 4 per cent in the summer and autumn months – a higher level than America's 1987 deficit. Merely a 'blip' or a 'problem of success' to the government, it was really an inevitable reflection of overvaluation, subsidising imports in the remorseless rise, the biggest increase in which was in consumer goods, particularly cars. The deficit required the pound to come down just as the dollar had fallen over 40 per cent from the heights of 1984–5. The Conservative government rejected that because inflation was their fear, not industrial decline and they were determined to protect money, not growth. Instead interest rates were raised to keep the pound up. The American solution of expanding production through a cheaper dollar and using the price mechanism against imports was eschewed. Britain did the exact opposite.

Instead Nigel Lawson opted for a high risk strategy of squeezing by high exchange rates which was certain to hit industry hard and threaten the nation with a repeat of the disaster of 1981, with rising unemployment, imports taking an even bigger share of its market and a new succession of closures in an industrial base already disastrously narrowed, all to keep up a pound whose overvaluation had caused the problem in the first place. If it succeeded we were paying foreigners high rates to bring in money to close a gap industry no longer could. If it failed the result was a run on sterling, a collapse and ever higher interest rates to shore it up. Money could leave as easily and as quickly as it had come. It would, when it judged that its interest rates gains were likely to be cancelled by a sterling fall. Either way, the mess was conclusive proof, if proof were needed at this, late, stage of the overwhelming importance of the thing the government had first pretended to ignore and then veiled in mystery – the exchange rate. Thanks to it, Britain was back in a worse version of the old balance of payments trap, at a lower level of employment, with a narrower industrial base, having largely squandered the oil which should have been used to save it.

Chapter 4
The Strange Death of
Industrial Britain

The exchange rate is crucial for manufacturing because price is crucial in competitive success or failure. British exchange rate policy had been grievously and consistently mishandled. These factors taken together provide the major explanation for Britain's unique industrial failure. It is not the single all-embracing cause, that would be too simplistic, but the long-term, conditioning factor undermining industry's prospects, boosting our competitors, making British industry increasingly vulnerable. In any murder mystery where one suspect is in every room in which a body is found, the causal relationships may be difficult to prove but the case looks well on the way to court.

So it is with exchange rates, though causal relationships can in fact be indicated by a detailed comparison between changes in competitiveness and key performance measures: economic growth, manufacturing production, the unemployment level and the balance of trade. For this purpose, the exchange rate is best measured as the 'real' exchange rate, not the nominal rate but the price at which our manufactured goods actually trade against competitors as measured by relative export unit values for all manufactures, and by the terms of trade against competitors in our market. These terms of trade tell us what is really happening in the UK market for finished manufactures, but they understate our loss of competitiveness by taking no account of goods no longer sold because they have been priced out – an important consideration in a country like Britain. Having lost two-thirds of our share of world trade and moved out of a number of fields, the terms of trade can make us seem more competitive than we are if account were taken of abandoned resources, skills, factories, and capacity, all of which need to be priced back into the markets from which they have been priced out. Table 2 covers as much of the period since the war as is possible on available figures. The figures are weighted to 1980, the indexes recalculated on 1975 because overvaluation then was much less than 1980, when the rise of the pound under monetarism had taken it to abnormal, and distorting, heights.

The broad pattern is depressingly clear. The UK share of the volume of manufactured exports falls and manufactured imports increase as the exchange rate rises. The last three columns show a close correlation between changes in competitiveness in columns 2 and 3 and trade performance, the earlier ones indicating a similar relation with the general state of the economy. As export unit values and the terms of trade rise, exports, output, employment and manufacturing production all fall in the next period. The sad saga of Britain's decline is there in graveyard columns. At the time, government and media saw specific crises, brought home by rises in unemployment (1975, 1981) or falls in output (1956, 1970, 1975, 1980) rather than the rise in the exchange rate which went before. What they did not see, because hidden by the pattern of stop and go, was the cumulative nature of the process. Unemployment rose to new, higher levels as manufacturing industry became unable to provide jobs. Interest rates also rose to higher levels to support the pound where manufacturing could not. The steady decline in our share of world trade reduced us to a level where the economy had to be kept underrun since we could no longer pay for increased imports by our exports. Any rise in the standard of living would have bankrupted the nation.

The terms of trade for finished manufactures increased (that is, became worse for manufacturing) during the 1950s. This was reflected in a fall in the volume of exports relative to imports in the last column, dwindling away to levels which only oil could finance by the eighties. The rise in relative export unit values in column 2, though not as marked as the increases in the terms of trade, reflects the damage done by the 'stops' of 1956, 1958 and 1960–1. The terms of trade rose more slowly in the 1960s than the fall in relative import values, but taking the decade as a whole, the fall in the UK share of MMC exports and the relative volume of exports to imports, both fell faster than in the fifties. It was the devaluation of 1967 which halted the fall in our share of the volume of MMC exports and prevented further deterioration in the relative volume of exports to imports. After sterling floated in June 1972, the UK share of the volume of MMC exports stayed at around 9 per cent and the volume of exports rose relative to imports in 1974 and 1975, an improvement more apparent than real because it reflected the fact that trade between the industrial countries fell most in the 1975 recession, and much of ours went elsewhere.

Table 2 The Exchange Rate and the UK Economy (1975 = 100).

	Terms Trade[1]	Export Price[2]	Unemployed %[3]	Int. Rate %[4]	Manf. Prod %	GDP %[5]	Share MMC[6]	Visible Balance of Trade[7]		
								less Oil & Errat.	Fin. less Err.	Manf. Rel. Vol.
1949			1.5					+2	+761	733
1950	80	93est	1.5	0.51	7.4	3.6	25.5	+129	+817	720
1951	84		1.2	0.56	3.0	1.8	21.9	−418	+951	502
1952	85	97	2.0	2.2	−5.0	0.6	21.5	−3	+952	448
1953	88	97	1.6	2.3	7.2	3.8	21.2	+10	+907	537
1954	88	97	1.3	1.8	5.4	4.2	20.3	+24	+982	475
1955	98	99	1.1	3.7	6.4	3.7	19.9	−56	+1061	466
1956	98	97	1.2	4.9	−0.3	1.2	19.4	+324	+1194	428
1957	92	98	1.4	4.8	2.4	1.6	18.4	+320	+1241	385
1958	92	101	2.1	4.6	0.9	−0.2	18.3	+362	+1257	326
1959	89	102	2.0	3.4	5.8	4.0	17.9	+233	+1258	244
1960	98	102	1.5	4.9	8.0	5.5	16.5	−51	+1239	246
1961	91	102	1.3	5.1	0.3	2.7	16.4	+220	+1308	225
1962	99	102	1.8	4.2	0.3	1.2	15.9	+288	+1311	230
1963	99	106	2.2	3.7	3.5	4.1	14.6	+278	+1479	189
1964	96	107	1.6	4.6	9.1	5.5	13.5	−61	+1359	196
1965	102	109	1.4	5.9	2.9	3.0	12.7	+243	+1518	184
1966	104	111	1.5	6.1	1.9	1.6	12.0	+406	+1632	145
1967	104	111	2.3	5.8	0.5	2.2	11.1	+13	+1350	141
1968	99	103	2.4	7.1	7.6	4.2	11.0	+4	+1544	147
1969	99	103	2.4	7.6	3.7	2.5	11.0	+552	+1858	136
1970	100	105	2.5	7.0	−0.4	1.9	10.2	+564	+1896	130
1971	101	106	2.8	5.6	−1.1	1.5	10.3	+1043	+2227	103
1972	102	107	3.1	5.5	2.2	2.4	9.5	+99	+1676	103
1973	95	98	2.1	9.3	9.3	7.3	9.5	−1360	+1177	90
1974	96	96	2.6	11.4	−1.2	−1.7	9.0	−1632	+1829	94

	Terms Trade[1]	Export Price[2]	Unem-ployed %[3]	Int. Rate %[4]	Manf. Prod %	GDP %[5]	Share MMC[6]	Visible Balance of Trade[7] less Oil & Errat.	Fin. less Err.	Manf. Rel. Vol.
1975	100	100	3.3	10.2	-6.9	-0.9	9.2	+461	+3626	100
1976	96	97	4.5	11.1	1.8	2.7	8.9	+168	+3633	96
1977	101	102	4.8	7.7	2.0	2.5	9.1	+928	+4022	90
1978	105	109	4.7	8.5	0.6	2.9	8.7	+471	+3127	78
1979	111	115	4.3	13.0	-0.2	2.7	8.2	-2598	+988	65
1980	118	129	5.4	15.1	-9.5	-2.3	7.9	+1529	+3107	67
1981	119	127	8.5	13.0	-6.0	-1.1	7.3	-163	+1652	62
1982	119	119	9.8	11.5	0.2	1.9	7.3	-3404	-574	57
1983	118	116	10.8	9.6	2.9	3.6	7.4	-9109	-474	48
1984	118	113	11.0	9.3	4.2	1.7	7.6	-12567	-5930	48
1985	118	115	11.2	11.6	2.4	3.8	7.7	-11194	-5301	49
1986	120	113	11.4	10.4	0.9	3.0	7.5	-14500	-7837	47
1987	121	117	10.2	9.2	5.8	4.3	7.8	-16462	-9004	47
1988	127	127	8.1	9.8	7.1	3.9e	7.3	-23828	-13876	40
1989[8]	128	133	7.0e	12.6	5.0e	3.4e	7.1e	-29000	-18000	38

Notes

1 Finished manufactures. Derived from *Monthly Review of External Statistics* and 11 March 1977 issue of *Trade and Industry*. UN figures before 1954.
2 Manufactures. From 1963 – IMF relative export unit values. Earlier figures derived from UN series.
3 After 1964 – unemployed claimants (excl. school leavers) as per cent of total working population including Armed Forces – gives lower figures.
4 Average of Treasury Bill rate.
5 At factor cost – average estimate.
6 Share of main manufacturing countries' exports of manufactures.
7 Cols 9–11 excl. erratics from 1970. Col. 9 – from 1970 Table A8 *MRETS*; for 1949–58 and 1964–9 Annual Abstracts; for 1959–63 Eurostat, but covers all fuel. Col. 10 – Table B2 less C2 of *MRETS* on OTS basis. Col. 11 from Table D3 *MRETS* from 1963 and *NIESR* Reviews 1950–62.
8 January 1989 estimated.

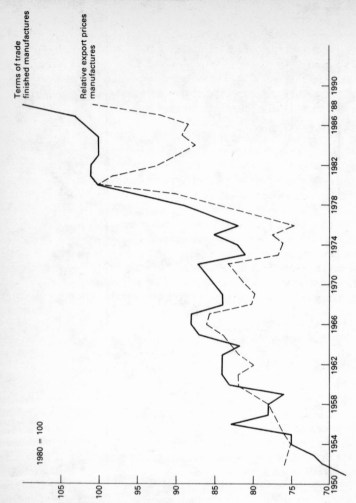

Figure 1   UK Relative Export Price for Manufactures and Terms of Trade for Finished Manufactures, 1950–88

There was still a massive decline in UK output and employment. The fall in the real exchange rate in the fourth quarter of 1976 was followed by an improvement in 1977, but unemployment was up by half on the 1972 peak and manufacturing output was still 5 per cent below the 1973 level. Since then, it has been downhill all the way.

Far from being the decade of recovery that the Conservative

government claims, for manufacturing it has been the period when slip became fall. The terms of trade turned against us even more severely than in the seventies. Relative unit values were higher, but oil allowed us to import more while producing less. So manufacturing production improved only round elections, while unemployment rose to new heights. The balance of trade in manufactures, in surplus through the seventies, moved into a deficit, unsupportable without oil. By 1988 even that could no longer fill the gap. British industry picked itself up from the depths of the monetarist recession as a result of the fall in relative export prices, largely due to the fall in the exchange rate. It has still not been able to win back any of the lost ground either in its home market or overseas.

The balance of trade column in Table 2 reflects the loss of the home market which British industry has always looked to for survival. Now it is losing that base which had kept it going, something which distinguishes Britain from her competitors. Imports now amount to more than half our output of finished manufactures, twice the level of other advanced countries. Where import penetration in 1968 was 17 per cent by 1985 it was 35 per cent, and this conceals the extent of the failure by including such industries as bricks and gravestone carving, which face lesser threats from abroad. Nor is this just a feature of any one sector of manufactured goods such as the producer goods which the government claims are being imported as investment rises, or the consumer goods Labour argues are flooding in because of the credit explosion and tax cuts. It is across the board. Consumer goods imports in 1988 were 76 per cent up on 1979. Intermediate goods were up 160 per cent as industry switched from domestic to overseas sources for the ingredients which go into its finished products, in order to cut costs. In capital goods the increase is 139 per cent, well over four times the 1973 figure. Manufacturing output in 1987 was still 4 per cent less than in 1973, and only recovered to that level in 1988. Britain had been the number three exporter of machine tools in 1960 but by the 1980s only had 5 per cent of the market. Our investment in plant and machinery is low compared to that of our competitors. Yet the whole of that investment, and more, now goes to imports. Such underlying trends point to a situation far more serious than any addiction to foreign cars. Industry, too, is becoming dependent. The problem is becoming built in.

Among the soaring amount of manufactured imports consumer goods have fared *least* disastrously. In 1988, the volume of imports was 76 per cent up on 1979 and 624 per cent up on 1970. Exports were up by 29 per cent and 78 per cent and production by 7 per cent and 29 per cent for those years, though the increase in both production and exports is suspect, since much of what is now produced in, and exported from, the UK comes from 'screw-driver' plants assembling Japanese products. The UK export figures may also include re-exports of home computers and other goods made in Taiwan and South Korea. The lower rise in consumer goods occurs only because they were higher already. Imports of consumer goods in 1970 were already equal to 61 per cent of exports in terms of value and by 1988 were 123 per cent higher. Imports of intermediate and capital goods likewise rose from, respectively, 50 per cent to 112 per cent and 45 per cent to 109 per cent, of exports.

As a result the deficit on the visible balance of trade at 1988 prices on an overseas trade statistics basis rose from £6.6 billion in 1970 to £25.2 billion in 1988. Similar figures are not available for oil, but net imports of crude oil in 1970 would have cost £5.7 billion at 1988 prices compared to net exports of £2.2 billion in 1988. The non-oil balance (on a balance of payments basis) has fallen from a surplus of £7.8 billion in 1970 (0.9 per cent of GDP) to a deficit of £22.7 billion in 1988, a turn-round of £30.5 billion. The overall visible deficit in 1988 was 4.4 per cent GDP, despite an oil contribution of 0.5 per cent. This is worse than that of the USA (3.7 per cent) at its worst in 1987. The decline in the balance of trade in manufactures, excluding erratic items, adds up to £37.3 billion, falling from a surplus of £18.6 billion in 1970 and £5.3 billion in 1979 to a deficit of £18.7 billion in 1988. Three-quarters of the decline – £27.9 billion – is accounted for by finished manufactures. There the balance of trade has fallen from a surplus of £14.0 billion in 1970 and £5.5 billion in 1979 to a deficit of £13.9 billion. The UK share of the value of exports of manufactures by the main manufacturing countries fell by 2.6 per cent between 1970 and 1987 compared to an increase in the German share of 1.6 per cent to 21.5 per cent. UK exports would have been at least £31 billion higher if we had done no more than hold our own in overseas markets – more than would be required to provide jobs for everyone. Here is the basic cause of Britain's failure – loss of jobs through loss of trade.

The loss of the home market is the worst part of the problem. It is across the board, affecting all sections of manufacturing as Table 3 reveals, and a country which cannot hold its own market cannot survive. There is no way manufacturing industry can do better in markets where it does not have the benefit of easy, cheap distribution, local pride, known brand names and longer standing networks; nor, given the costs of distribution and exporting, can it make sufficient profits from foreign markets to rebuild in Britain. History points the other way: more profit should be made at home with less coming from exports. Manufacturing cannot even pay for the imports which now gnaw at its base. Indeed, in many areas manufacturing is itself becoming an importer just to stay in business.

The stages of this deterioration underline its causes. The increase in import penetration between 1968 and 1970, following the 1967 devaluation was small. It became sharper between 1970 and 1973, particularly in motor cars and electrical products, due in part to the increase in the real exchange rate before sterling was floated in June 1972, in part to the rush by continental manufacturers to strengthen their position in the UK market, and in part to the big

Table 3 Imports of Manufactures as a Percentage of Home Demand

	1968	1970	1973	1975	1979	1982	1987
All manufactures	17	17	21	22	27	29	35
Chemicals	18	18	22	25	30	33	40
Motor vehicles	5	7	23	29	41	47	48
Textiles	16	15	21	26	33	39	46
Clothing and footwear	12	13	18	26	29	33	38
Food and drink	21	19	19	18	18	16	18
Metal goods	5	6	10	11	10	12	17
Mechanical eng.	20	20	26	29	29	39	38
Electrical eng.*	14	17	27	32	31	40	48
Office/Data process				71	92	105	101
Instruments	30	32	46	54	53	56	57

1968–73 are not fully comparable
*1968–73 includes office machinery etc

increase in UK demand from the Barber boom. Imports (excluding erratic items) rose 58 per cent – nearly six times faster than UK output. Import penetration increased by another 4.3 per cent between 1973 and 1979, the greater part after sterling was uncapped in 1977. Manufacturing output fell 4 per cent between 1973 and 1979, while imports rose by 53 per cent and exports by 19 per cent. The combination of deflation and free trade was disastrous.

The rate of decline since 1979 has been even faster: 9.1 per cent in eight years compared to 8.7 per cent in the previous eleven. In 1987, manufacturing output was only 1 per cent higher than in 1979, but imports, excluding the erratic items, were up by 70 per cent and exports by only 25 per cent. Output was 5 per cent higher in the food and drink industries, but down by 54 per cent in the case of man-made fibres, 21 per cent in motor vehicles, 19 per cent in mechanical engineering, 16 per cent in miscellaneous metal manufacturing, 15 per cent in textiles, 11 per cent in metals and 6 per cent in clothing and footwear. Most of the damage has been done by imports from the EEC. Their share of our market rose from 6 per cent in 1970 to 20 per cent in 1987. The share of the rest of the world rose only from 11 to 15 per cent.

The sorry story can be illustrated by the Lancashire cotton industry. This was the first example of growth based on specialisation the world has ever seen and in 1913 it exported 7,075 million linear yards of cotton cloth, more than 80 per cent of its total output. Mass production industries relying on volume sales at a comparatively low unit margin of profit are the first to be hit by overvaluation. The Lancashire textile industry is the classic case of an industry which was successful because of economies of scale, with whole mills producing a single type of yarn or cloth, but which was torpedoed by exchange rate policies – first the return to gold in 1925, then the steady appreciation after the Second World War. The steady increase in relative export prices caused production of spun and woven cotton, man-made fibre and mixture cloth to fall (in linear terms) from 2,587 million yards in 1949 to 1,612 million yards in 1958, 1,136 million yards in 1970 and a derisory 492 million metres in 1987. Exports of cotton cloth fell from 903 million yards in 1949 to 384 million square yards in 1958, 123 million square yards in 1970, and 126 million metres in 1987. Employment fell from 310,000 in 1949 and 165,000 in 1970 to only 30,000 in 1987. In 1913 it had been 670,000.

The UK was just not competitive in an industry where almost everything depends on price. The situation grew worse when we joined the EEC with the UK production of cotton cloth falling 60 per cent between 1970 and 1986 compared with an increase of 18 per cent in Italy and a fall of only 7 and 22 per cent respectively in Germany and France (see Table 4).

Table 4 Production of Cotton Cloth (thousand tonnes)

	UK	Germany	France	Italy
1949	287	145	173	110
1959	191	275	215	120
1970	90	182	165	175
1986	36	169	128	206

The decline is generally attributed to imports from low-cost countries and ironically the UK textile industry backed the campaign to push Britain into the Common Market. In the event,

Lancashire lost far more from greater imports from the EEC than anything it may have gained by increased protection against imports from the developing countries. Imports from the EEC of cotton and man-made fibre cloth quadrupled between 1970 and 1987 and were one-fifth higher than domestic production increasing from 150 million square yards to 593 million square metres. Imports from other countries doubled from an estimated 480 million square yards to 1,005 million square metres. Imports of cotton cloth from the EEC more than doubled between 1979 and 1987.

The Germans and others do not view textiles as a sunset industry. In 1987, UK imports of cotton cloth from the founder members of the EEC amounted to 157 million square metres. UK exports in return amounted to only 46 million square metres. UK imports of grey, loom-state cloth from Germany and the Netherlands amounted to 50 million square metres. They bought only 9 million square metres from us. An industry exporting 80 per cent of its output in 1913 has been all but wiped out; its dark, satanic job-creating mills now used as warehouses for imported goods, its finishers now kept going by processing imports of grey cloth from the developing countries.

Imports of man-made fibres for use in the textile industry have increased from 43 per cent of the UK market in 1979 to 67 per cent in 1987. UK production in 1987 fell to 46 per cent of the 1979 figure and 37 per cent of the 1973 peak. In 1970, exports of man-made fibres were worth 3.5 times the value of imports, in 1979 they were only double, and in 1987 the value of imports was 12 per cent higher than that of exports, a deterioration almost entirely due to increased imports from the EEC. In 1970, exports of man-made fibres to the EEC were worth 2.8 times the value of imports. In 1987, the value of imports from the EEC was 64 per cent higher than the value of exports to it. The figures include trade in rayon, where the residual production not controlled by Courtaulds remains in the EEC. In 1987, imports were worth 2.7 times the value of exports to the EEC and whole plants have been closed down in Northern Ireland to concentrate production on the continent.

The whole textile industry has been hard hit. The share of the UK market taken by imports rose from 15 per cent in 1970 to 33 per cent in 1979, and 46 per cent in 1987. Jobs are down from 715,000 in 1970 to 450,000 in 1979 and 244,000 in 1987 – a loss of 472,000 in seventeen years, one-sixth of the 3 million jobs lost in manufacturing over the same period.

The EEC share of imports has risen from 43 per cent in 1970 to 58 per cent in 1979 and 67 per cent in 1987, increasing the EEC share of the UK market from 6 per cent in 1970 to 17 per cent in 1979 and 29 per cent in 1987. The share taken by other countries has only risen by 8 per cent, from 9 per cent in 1970, to 16 per cent in 1979, to 17 per cent in 1987. The relative value of exports to imports from the EEC has fallen from 105 per cent in 1970 to 71 per cent in 1979, and to only 44 per cent in 1987. The surplus of £7 million in trade with the EEC in textiles turned into a deficit of £248 million in 1979 and £1,258 million in 1987; enough trade to solve the problem of unemployment in scores of textile towns.

Yet textiles have done all that government demanded: unions are weak, pay is low, round the clock shift-working is common, work loads are heavy. Prices rose 13 per cent less than the retail price index between 1970 and 1986 despite a much larger increase in input costs. Wholesale and export prices rose by 337 per cent and 332 per cent respectively, compared with 385 per cent for raw materials and fuel, 457 per cent for hourly earnings of full-time adult male workers and 682 per cent for females, who make up the bulk of the workforce. All of this is to no avail because of the increase in the real exchange rate.

The story can be repeated in many other less well documented cases. Now, jobs could be recovered faster by making good the ground lost in older industries than by trying to develop new ones. At least a million of our working population – particularly those in the ethnic minorities – have acquired the necessary skills, machinery can quickly be installed, capacity rebuilt, so why give up these industries for dead? All that is required is a reduction in UK prices in terms of foreign currencies by a fall in the exchange rate. Yet in June 1988 the nominal rate for sterling was 15 per cent higher (at 78.7) than in the fourth quarter of 1986. The corresponding figure for export unit values was a crippling 22 per cent, no less than 42 per cent higher than in the fourth quarter of 1976. The increases against our principal competitors were:

	4Q 1986	4Q 1976
USA	35%	39%
Germany	17%	44%
Japan	13%	26%
EEC Six	13%	39%

This explains why we buy more than twice as much from the Germans as they buy from us. Pundits urge industry up-market or into niches, but neither way answers the problem of an overvalued exchange rate. Nor is mechanisation the solution at a time of falling output – it only accelerates job losses. Output per head doubled in the British textile industry between 1970 and 1986 but did no good because production was halved. Three out of four workers lost their jobs. Investment is low and shuttleless looms are only a third as numerous as in Italy and Germany. Yet what good purpose is served by substituting capital for labour where a fall in the exchange rate would reduce costs more effectively?

Bringing down the price through adjusting the currency and easing the burden of interest rates is the only way to increase output and employment. Most of what we import from the EEC could be produced here. It is not – because of economic policies on interest and exchange rates, not because of the inadequacy of the industry.

Textile manufacture and the industries it typifies show that an overvalued exchange rate dooms industry, but that if alleviated it can respond, as it did in 1973 and 1985–7, with rises in output, a surge of productivity, an improvement in exports, better performance on the home market and improved profits. Yet each year the room for manoeuvre becomes less. Total manufacturing output exceeded the peak of the second quarter of 1974 only in the second quarter of 1988. Imports of finished manufactures as a proportion of UK output rose from 9 per cent in 1966 to 27.5 per cent in 1976 and 48 per cent in 1984 and are now 54 per cent. Corresponding figures for Germany (26 per cent), France (28 per cent) and Italy (24 per cent) were all far lower. Even after the recent recovery manufacturing output is only 25 per cent up on 1981, imports are 100 per cent up.

It has also taken a down turn in its level of employment and economic activity. Both have fallen becoming locked into permanent under capacity. Once capacity is closed and jobs lost, the economy becomes locked into its reduced level. Attempts to expand are checked by an import and inflation barrier. The attempt itself becomes increasingly unlikely. Manufacturing now provides only a quarter of employment, so its voice is weaker. Those with vested interests in imports, to which consumers are becoming addicted, in assembly of imports, in the EEC itself, and the overwhelming interest of finance, are all much stronger. A coalition for decline takes power. Finance is a worldwide interest independent of the industrial base. A land which could succeed begins to doubt its ability to do so again. It is told by siren voices that it doesn't need to bother. Such are the symptoms of decline – not new life but industrial rigor mortis.

Chapter 5
Towards a Solution

Britain's engine of growth has lost 3 million jobs, and at least a quarter of its wealth-creating potential as the workshop of the world has become its back-street garage. It cannot produce the wealth, pay its way in the world, provide the jobs, or generate the growth which improves the lot of the people and sustains the surplus for public spending. Britain and socialism both face a gloomy future unless we can rebuild the economy and provide the jobs. That means regaining the ground lost in our own and overseas markets.

We will not do this by present methods. Unsustainable growth has taken us back to stop–go because the Conservative government has opted for one-legged, privatised Keynesianism, boosting consumer demand, not production, opting for high interest rates and, therefore, a high exchange rate. All this has been harmful to British industry and the end result has been to bring back the old stop–go with a higher level of unemployment and a narrower industrial base. Tory economics has taken ten years to demonstrate its futility, inflicting incalculable damage in the process.

There are several currently fashionable alternatives. Sadly, each produces new problems. A massive boost to public spending as Labour promised at the last election would merely wash overseas to the advantage of competitors without concentrating the benefits on areas of greatest need. Collective economic expansion in the advanced economies would do nothing to improve our relative weakness because it takes no account of our propensity to import compared with others. It might even heighten it by benefiting stronger economies disproportionately. International coordination of exchange rates is popular but nations do not abandon self-interest when they sit round conference tables, and no international forum has tackled the unbalanced trading caused by the persistent undervaluation of the D-Mark and the yen. Both must go up if the world is to trade fairly. Yet international cooperation has been dedicated to stopping the dollar coming down so competitors could continue to loot the American market. Cooperation on this basis is pure hypocrisy yet anything more principled is attempting to make water run uphill.

There is no evidence that trade is diminished by volatility. Even if there were, stability would not benefit Britain. What is good for exporters would be equally good for importers, and we import more than we export. The problem is the valuation. Day to day, or even year to year, changes in nominal exchange rates are nothing compared to the damage inflicted by prolonged overvaluation or the benefits of prolonged undervaluation. Both are national decisions. Since there is no international organisation dedicated to giving national *aegrotats*, or to helping lame economies across Market Street, only national decisions can change things. The world is a struggle of competing self-interests. We have failed because we lost sight of ours and as the consequences of that neglect now verge on disaster, we can only look to our own efforts to avert them. Competitors are perfectly happy for us to go downhill if they benefit, but the consequence of British recovery would be to make life tougher for the economies which have done so well at our expense. Economic competition is not a zero sum game. World trade expands. Demand is insatiable. Yet in any manufacturing investment period, or any electoral cycle, British resurgence comes partially at the expense of the competition, just as America's industrial recovery is damaging our exports.

It must be ourselves alone, or nothing. We cannot control our own destinies but we can influence them. The only requirement is techniques that work. Here the nation-building experiences of industrialising countries offer relevant examples. As do the market methods which have stimulated the growth of Silicon Valley out of California's dynamism. Or the cooperation between state and private sector which rebuilt Boston and shifted Japan to the new information-based industries. What is needed are systems that work not theories.

Total change is appropriate only in a *tabula rasa*, and dirigiste methods are counter-productive in an economy where markets, incentives and the profit motive are central. On the other hand, Mrs Thatcher's hands off approach has also failed because it is irrelevant to an economy which is declining, vulnerable and exposed. Again practicality is the test. It is not market capitalism which has failed, but government's refusal to allow the market to operate in the crucial area of exchange rates. It was not intervention that produced the problems before but its one-sided nature. Proclaiming 'all state' or 'all market' is equally fatal, both must cooperate. The main weight of any policy needs to be free market, for prices and markets motivate now and we compete in a market world. Yet markets have to be managed and the State is not the remote alien force of Mrs Thatcher's imagination, but the community in action, our bulwark against the world, the agent of coordination, an instigating force, the manager of markets – just as it has been for our competitors.

Post-war decline and the failure of the Thatcher government were both due to misuse of the exchange rate. A combination of management and market can provide the competitive exchange rate Britain has rarely had. Without competitiveness and the profits it sustains, there can be no investment, no rebuilding, and domestic expansion is brief and benefits competitors, as Mitterrand's of 1982 and Reagan's from 1982 to 1985 both did. In our economy with its high propensity to import, unmanaged expansion will benefit British industry only minimally. So the economy must be insulated in order to expand, and in this respect the exchange rate is the key to both competitiveness and insulation. It must come down and be kept down to encourage investment, allow it to pay off and build a new dynamic into the economy.

Mrs Thatcher views competitiveness as an 'easy' answer because she sees tough solutions as virtuous, even if wrong. In fact it can offer the chance of hard work for real results as opposed to hard, miserable work on the treadmill of decline. Competitiveness is not the answer but the opportunity; the lever which gives priority to manufacturing jobs and growth, and restricts it for money, finance and inertia. It will not work automatically or on its own. Other measures must be coupled with it but no measure at all will work without it. It is a necessary, but not sufficient, condition for Britain's rebirth, the main instrument which still remains available to us and the only one which allows us to reverse the failures of the last forty years, because it caused them in the first place.

Some hold that the exchange rate lever will no longer work. Huge flows of money are far bigger than trade and its payments and far, far bigger than official reserves. Even if combined these are less than the money flows during a couple of days, so exchange markets are dominated by capital movements and exchange rates no longer move to balance trade flows but in response to speculative flows, geared to interest rates and valuation prospects as between major economies. They now exacerbate trade imbalances rather than correct them; a rising currency overshoots, a falling one falls more than it needs to. So how can governments control the exchange rate? They can't but they *can* influence it. In Britain they always have done, while pretending not to. Certainly they must now that the rate has become more and more dependent on those market flows. Just because the Conservatives have made the economy more dependent and exposed, there is no reason why we should not break out of the trap.

The rate can be talked up – or down, as the Americans did theirs in 1987, and as we should have done in 1980–1 or in 1976–7. The rate reflects government priorities and their economic consequences: expansion, the balance of payments, the tightness of credit, all of which can be changed appropriately affecting the prospects of the economy. Last, and most important of all, interest rates are the basic tool; put them up, up goes the pound; down, and it falls. Government controls interest rates. Under this government ours have been high in comparison with both competitors and the past – usually double (on Treasury Bills) the rate in Germany, a third higher than the USA. The excuses change: high American interest rates, high public sector borrowing, 'bearing down on inflation'. One by one all have gone. The high rates remain because government wants them that way. It wants them because it represents finance and it wants the pound where they put it. The record says that high interest rates and an overvalued pound are central to the strategies of this government. There are endless hopes of a reduction but the real move is upward most of the time, which means ruin for the real economy because price is the crucial factor in competitive mass markets. The currency influences this directly, subsidising exports, taxing imports when overvalued, doing the opposite when competitive. Sophisticates argue the price is now unimportant, 'non-price' factors like quality and design are now far more significant. Yet every aspect of a product has a cost; price and non-price competitiveness are on the same continuum. Unless a product is price competitive it can't gain a place on the market from which to build. Price is essential to mastery of production and, through it, of markets and without profits, arising from price competitiveness, there is nothing available to spend to improve all the 'non-price' factors which is why British industry has fallen so far behind. Mrs Thatcher sees success as 'producing the goods people want at the price they want to pay', a truism breathtaking in its stupidity. Like the tourist finding his way to Dublin, Britain does not start from there. Stand Mrs Thatcher's argument on its head: use devaluation to bring down prices and generate higher profits, then seize the opportunity of that exchange rate competitiveness and the profit flow it generates to improve investment, production and productivity, design, R and D, delivery and everything else. Unless we kick-start the engine of growth we are doomed to a losing struggle and ultimate defeat at the hands of those who have used devaluation in the past to expand to a scale where Mrs Thatcher's exhortations are actually relevant.

Devaluation is not subject to retaliation, as would be the case with import controls or tariffs. We are no longer a major player and so can act more independently, seizing the opportunity to pursue our own interests as others have rather than feeling an obligation to Boy Scout duty. Indeed, the increased cost of raw materials does not preclude devaluation; Britain lives by value added. Devaluation increases the potential for it and puts up the price of imported food and basic materials. Yet they account for less than one-fifth of imports. Three-quarters are manufactured goods – someone else's added value; someone else's jobs.

It influences the multinationals as nothing else can. Socialists dislike these giant organisations, mainly because the first wave and the biggest were American owned. Yet beggars can't be choosers. A country which has not sustained its own producers to the point where it now needs jobs, investment, and research and development desperately needs multinationals to widen the manufacturing base and to link Britain with the world, provided they use Britain as a base to export from and not just a market to exploit. We should do deals, ensuring investment in and exports from this country in return for access to our market and a profitable base to work from.

Bullying and bended knees are equally silly. Talk turkey instead. Government has three coins to trade: regional aid, access to our market, a competitive base to export from. The latter is crucial. Multinationals first came when a British base gave access to the imperial market. With EEC membership and overvaluation there was less incentive to stay, or for new ones to come, and organisations like Ford, GM, Kodak, Sony, IBM, and Philips, transferred their weight to the Continent. Cars for Britain were sourced from there. Ford publicly, others privately, made it clear that further investment in their British operations was unlikely as long as overvaluation continued, others eased out. As the pound came down Ford, GM and Peugeot brought in more investment – producing more cars here, making a bigger contribution to their international operations from here – Nissan came, Electrolux bought in. The investment tide was returning because Britain had become a profitable base for multinationals. Renewed overvaluation now reverses that just as the crucial discussions on investment for the Single Market are made.

The deterioration in manufactured trade since 1970 is £37 billion at current prices. This more than accounts for the increase in unemployment over the period and that happens because it is markets we have lost. We can only win them back by market methods. Price has defeated us. So change it by seizing the opportunity of competitiveness. Financial interests will greet the change with hysteria. The exchange rate has been consistently used to benefit them. We would be using it for people and for different social priorities. Internationalists, like the Foreign Office represent foreigners and so will protest loudly. They should realise that only a strong economy can enable Britain to make a strong contribution internationally. Devaluation is the natural remedy because competitiveness is now the precondition of survival. Used as a tool, in combination with a concerted strategy for growth, it offers a better prospect for rebuilding than any other combination – probably the only one.

Why then are politicians and pundits so doubtful about it? The fear is that a fall in the exchange rate must raise the rate of inflation, unless accommodated by a fall in living standards. Yet this is a textbook proposition which assumes that the increase in production made possible by a fall in the exchange rate will be less than required to correct the imbalance of trade, and that government cannot redistribute the benefits of the improvement to compensate anyone who loses out. Both assumptions are wrong. The argument is that a rise in import prices will result in the same rise in all prices. This 'Law of One Price' was popularised in the seventies by Terry Burns and the so-called International Monetarists. Yet they never explained how the theory could fit a country whose currency was overvalued and whose prices were, therefore, too high anyway. The reality is that any link between domestic prices and world prices – which also underlies the Purchasing Power Parity Theory of exchange rates – is at best tenuous, even in internationally traded goods. Prices vary considerably between one country and another. Firms price to markets not to production. Neither law is relevant, much as both have comforted those responsible for Britain's decline.

Inflation is too much money chasing too few goods. However, it does not follow that the problem is best solved by reducing the supply of money. In conditions of less than full employment the optimum solution must be to increase the supply of goods. An increase in output reduces unit costs in real terms at every level from central government downwards.

A fall in the exchange rate will raise wages and prices in export and import-competing industries, but this must be welcomed. The price of thousands of items once produced in this country, but now imported, must rise to make it profitable to produce them here again. Those industries must attract good workers. UK manufacturers need to increase their profit margins to invest. Yet the price of manufactures generally would not rise by anything like the full amount of the devaluation because importers would hold their prices as long as possible to retain market share, and the movement in costs would not be all one way. Economies of scale come as output increases, interest rate burdens would fall and unit costs come down with increased production. In the USA unit labour costs rose 29 per cent in the three years to 1982 as production fell. Consumer prices rose 33 per cent. In March 1988, units costs were 8 per cent less than in January 1983. Consumer prices were up by 17 per cent despite an increase in producer prices of only 5 per cent. Expansion made that possible.

What matters at the end of the day is the standard of living, not the cost. The real problem of inflation is one of income distribution. The UK suffers because a large slice of the money available is in too few hands. That deprives the masses and stimulates pay pressures, but the larger the size of the economic cake, the easier to divide it between competing groups without making any group worse off, or exciting that intense competition which generates inflation. What is needed is an increase in take-home pay, helped by a reduction in the burden of tax and national insurance to distribute the inevitable increase in real, disposable national income equitably.

A fall in the exchange rate does not add to the supply of money but reduces it, being, if anything, deflationary because of the wealth effect in terms of foreign currencies. It can give rise to inflation only if employers and employees take advantage of the resulting increase in demand to raise prices, or wages, by more than is required to attract the additional capital and labour required to meet it; an objection which applies equally to any increase in demand, in so far as it applies at all. It is argued that the economic benefits would be short-lived, that prices would rise and with real wages equal to money wages divided by prices, real wages would fall. Money wages would therefore rise to compensate, leading to even higher prices and inflation, so that quite early on the competitive advantage from the fall in the exchange rate would be lost to higher inflation. Yet devaluation has not done this in the UK. There has been no reduction of real wages after any devaluation. Neither did it occur in the USA nor in Sweden where hourly earnings have consistently risen faster than prices over the four years since devaluation, despite the fall in unemployment respectively from 10.6 to 5.4 per cent and 3.5 to 1.7 per cent. More people, in each case, are enjoying higher, real wages.

The Cambridge Economic Policy Group put the case differently: real wages would need to fall to accommodate an increase in profits. This is not true either. The share of real wages would fall, but that is a very different proposition and an effect cancelled by the bigger cake. Devaluation would push up profits faster than wages. However, some of the increase in profits would be taken in tax and thus be made available for distribution, some would be spent on investment, and hence jobs and a proportion of the increase in profits would be saved. Much of industry is now owned by pension funds and savings institutions accumulating funds, while companies would strengthen balance sheets by increasing cash balances or repaying debt. If there really is a problem, the answer is to neutralise this increase in saving by raising Corporation Tax and redistributing it to those who will spend.

Expansion will increase both profits and real wages simply because the cake is bigger. It will do so directly and, by reducing the cost to the public of unemployment, indirectly. To be effective any strategy for tackling unemployment must make manufactured imports more expensive than domestic production. The choice is in the means, not the end. It could be done by raising the price of imports in terms of sterling by pushing down the exchange rate or imposing tariffs, or allowing competition from imports to reduce costs and prices in industry so as to make our goods and services cheaper. Devaluation is better. It creates the opportunity for increasing output in order to bring down unit costs and spreads the burdens across the whole community rather than concentrating them on industry and labour. The present government has chosen the exchange rate as the engine of deflation, not because that approach is better but because it disciplines industry and unions and because Conservative voters gain more than they lose from overvaluation. These gains are won at terrible cost. Deflation places the burden of price adjustment on industries producing goods and services which are traded internationally. Anything which weakens them weakens the economy. When they lose heart and hope, their resources of labour and capital move elsewhere. The alternative is to say that we dare not reduce unemployment because the effect on living standards of the employed would be damaging. This is not an argument Labour could accept, neither is it true. Policies which create jobs raise the standard of living of the overwhelming majority by easing the burden of unemployment. The resource cost of employing people is not much greater than the cost of making them idle. So everyone gains when the unemployed are put back to work.

The theoretical arguments against devaluation are not borne out by the evidence. Britain's experience of post-war devaluations – two by the Conservatives and three by Labour – shows this (Table 5). Such an analysis does not lack faults. Figures are published in calendar years but devaluations are not appropriately timed to correspond. Economists relegate what they don't like to the dog-pound of *ceteris paribus*, but in the real world oddities wander the landscape such as the Korean War, nine months after the 1949 devaluation. Nevertheless in 1949, prices rose by 3.4 per cent up to September. The corresponding figure a year later was 2.2 per cent, despite the outbreak of the Korean War in June. The current account balance moved from a deficit of £1 million to a surplus of £307 million, a figure not surpassed until 1958. Real expenditure on goods and services at market prices rose by 3.2 per cent, real personal disposable incomes by 3.0 per cent, and real consumers' expenditure by 2.7 per cent. Unemployment stayed at an almost irreducible 1.5 per cent.

In 1968, the increase in retail prices was 4.7 per cent, the same as three years before. Real expenditure rose by 4.7 per cent, real personal disposable incomes by 1.8 per cent and real consumers' expenditure by 2.8 per cent. Unemployment was 2.4 per cent while profits rose and investment which depended on them reached a peak in 1970.

The rise in prices in the mid-seventies was accompanied by a fall in the nominal exchange rate. The one was not caused by the other any more than the rise in prices in the early 1980s was caused by the accompanying increase in the nominal exchange rate, but the contrast is revealing. External pressures of higher food, fuel and basic material prices were much greater in 1973 than in 1980. Yet real consumers' expenditure rose by 4.7 per cent in 1973 and fell by 3.0 per cent in 1980. Real disposable incomes rose by 6.8 per cent in 1973 compared to 1.8 per cent in 1980 – after increases in the previous year of 8.5 and 5.4 per cent respectively. Real consumers' expenditure rose by 6.1 per cent and 0.3 per cent respectively. Again, profits and investment both rose. The fall in UK interest rates, and in sterling, in 1982–3 and again in the devaluation of 1986–7, were each followed by increases in output, reductions in the rate of inflation and a rise in living standards. UK manufacturers absorbed the whole of the increase in their labour costs between January 1986 and August 1987.

Table 5 Britain's Devaluations

	Cripps 1949	Callaghan 1967	Barber 1973	Healey 1976	Lawson 1986
Devaluation (%)[1]					
Nominal	30	14.3	16.1	16.9	16.9
Export prices (IMF)	11	10.5	13.9	8.2	11.4
Export prices (DTI)	n.a.	10.8	14.3	9.9	11.1
Trade weighted	11	n.a.	9.4	14.3	7.4
Rel. exp. unit	n.a.	6.4	7.7	3.5	2.4
Trade Balance (£m)					
Previous year	n.a.	1,632	1,674	3,312	−5,307
That year	761	1,350	1,177	3,570	−7,837
Next year	817	1,544	1,828	3,915	−9,004
Second year	951	1,858	3,312	2.980	−13,876
Vol. of Exports					
Previous year	90	102	90	96	100
That year	100	100	100	100	100
Next year	114	114	107	104	109
Second year	115	129	112	104	133
Vol. of Imports					
Previous year	93	82	79	91	95
That year	100	100	100	100	100
Next year		116	103	112	106
Second year		127	97	129	113
Manufacturing Output					
Previous year	94.0	99.4	91.6	98.0	99.2
That year	100	100	100	100	100
Next year	106.8	107.1	98.8	101.9	111
Second year	111.4	111.1	91.9	102.3	
Economic Growth					
Previous year	n.a.	1.8	3.3	−0.9	3.8
That year	3.5	2.4	7.2	2.7	3.2
Next year	3.4	3.9	−1.9	2.4	4.3
Second year	2.1	2.6	−0.9	3.5	3.9
Weekly Earnings					
Previous year	93.8	96.8	87.8	86.5	92.7
That year	100	100	100	100	100
Next year	105.2	108.5	117.5	109.1	107.7
Second year	117.2	116.5	149.0	123.2	117

continued overleaf

Table 5 – *continued*

	Cripps 1949	Callaghan 1967	Barber 1973	Healey 1976	Lawson 1986
Prices					
Previous year	97.2	97.6	91.6	85.5	96.7
That year	100	100	100	100	100
Next year	102.8	104.8	116.0	115.9	104.1
Second year	112.8	110.4	124.2	125.5	
Share MMC Trade					
(% vol.)	26	11.1	9.5	8.9	7.5

Note

[1] Trade figures are for finished manufactures. The export price figures are unit values covering 3Q67 to 1Q68, 2Q72 to 4Q73, 1976, 1Q83, and 3Q85 to 4Q86.

Inflationary consequences were minimal. Unit costs came down with increased production. Interest rates came down with sterling. The standard of living improved because resources and workers previously unemployed or underemployed were brought back into production. It is deflation which increases inflation and cuts the standard of living. British devaluations have done the opposite and been successful. The degree of success depends on the level of unemployed resources: the greater the underused capacity of machines, services and men, the more slack there is to take in, the greater the need for devaluation and the greater the benefits. The lesson is clear: overvaluation is harmful to an industrial economy, devaluation a stimulus.

American experience in the eighties reinforces the same lesson. Manufactured imports more than doublèd as the value of the dollar doubled. The American share of MMC exports of manufactures fell from 17 per cent in 1980 (the same as 1970) to 14 per cent in 1986, in volume terms less than 12 per cent. The American deficit on visible trade, on a balance of payments basis, rose from $40 billion in 1979 (when the dollar was just about holding its own against the D-Mark and the yen for the first time since 1949) to $144 billion in 1986. As the dollar came down there was a dramatic industrial revival, a surge of exports in volume terms, and only a small increase in the rate of inflation to 3.8 per cent. Unit labour costs in manufacturing in the year to March 1988 hardly increased over the preceding twelve months.

If the benefits from Britain's devaluations – all too little too late – most forced, not wanted – are as substantial as they have been, and if the penalties of overvaluation are so great, then the lesson is obvious. We must begin to use the exchange rate for our own purposes, instead of being used by it.

Chapter 6
Mastering Money

In the 1930s, recognising that mass unemployment was a monetary not a trade phenomenon, the National government set out to stop instabilities by asserting its control over the financial system. The post-war period has seen a long retreat from that position. National controls were relaxed or eliminated until only interest-rates were left. World coordination through the Bretton Woods system crumbled. Finance threw off its shackles and restraints nationally and internationally and became more powerful than governments. British Ministers basked in its praise, worshipped at its altars. By the late seventies, previous relationships had been so far reversed that finance took control behind the front of a Conservative government which represented money and those who manipulated it, established its religion, monetarism in power and set out to make Britain's little world fit for finance to live in.

Industry declined *pari passu*. Its needs, cheap money and a competitive currency, have never been fulfilled because of the power of finance. It suffered from the increasing instabilities unregulated finance generates. Enormous, fast, financial flows produced dramatic fluctuations in exchange rates which unsettled industry while prolonged overshoots destroyed it. The increasing possibility of plummeting falls put governments at the mercy of the financiers, making them anxious to propitiate the merchants of greed. Industry carried the can for all this. It was punished for the problems – overheating, asset inflation, credit explosion – which finance had certainly caused. Industry cannot live comfortably in a house in which finance is king and finance's return to the throne was followed once again by mass unemployment, always the result of financial failures and instabilities and not the problem of production.

This is why expansionary government must make money its servant, not its master. Money is neither a mystery nor a sacred object; just a medium which must be put to work for growth and jobs rather than the selfish purposes of the merchants of greed. What has been done by the decline in spending on British production, as a result of the failures of government and the central bank, can be undone, but only with power over money.

That power, and its effect on the currency, is now one of the few means of national economic management available, but it confers the vital ability to manage our economic relations with the outside world and regulate their effects on our economy through the exchange rate. Of all the weapons of insulation used in the thirties' devaluation, or to put it in market terms, using the price mechanism to adjust the terms of trade, alone remains available to strengthen the economy. Of all the weapons of the fifties to cushion and comfort an underproductive people, overvaluation – buying more imports for less domestic production – alone remains as the economy weakens.

The need to keep that national control over the exchange rate is why entry to the Exchange Rate Mechanism of the European Monetary System would be disastrous for the nation, and particularly for any government dedicated to expansion. Membership is urged by the Democrats, the CBI and their backing chorus of naive pundits and papers and groups on two grounds. It would make us more communautaire and allow us to influence the development of a European currency and bank and the general financial shape of the EEC as 1992 approaches. Secondly, it would stop fluctuations and volatility which endanger trade. The first argument is valueless and was urged for Britain's initial entry. It has harmed us and brought us little influence and forced us to play Europe's sulky child. The argument is always plunge in further and it will get better, but it never does. There is more to be gained by controlling our own destinies, sensibly, for our own purposes than by becoming a minor voice with little influence in institutions weighted against us. The second argument is baseless. If stability helps trade then it harms us, since as net importers we lose out. Yet no study shows that fluctuations have ever damaged trade. The real problem is overvaluation and that would be made worse by tying sterling to a D-Mark which needs to go up if the world is to trade fairly. Germany's huge surplus is Europe's problem. It is produced by an undervalued exchange rate used as a protective device. Since the exchange rate is a market-clearing mechanism, in a country suffering from mass unemployment it must be overvalued if an increase in the rate of growth leads to balance of payments crisis, as has happened in Britain. In a country enjoying a growing balance of payments surplus, the exchange rate must be undervalued if an increase in the growth rate simply increases the surplus – as in Germany's case, where this is happening already. The huge trade surpluses of Germany and Japan are causing a dangerous world disequilibrium and this can only be solved by substantial revaluations of the D-Mark and the yen, allowing the world to trade fairly. Japan, a country more susceptible to American pressures and nervous of its trading position, has been accommodating and allowed the real value of the yen to appreciate by 32 per cent since 1985, double the appreciation of the D-Mark. They have also done far more to increase demand at home. So the Japanese share of exports of manufactures has actually fallen from 19.7 to 18.1 per cent. Germany has selfishly powered ahead increasing its share from 18.7 to 21.5 per cent on the back of an undervalued D-Mark, which the EMS helps to keep down. The world and Europe need an increase in prices of German goods to make them less competitive. Instead the EMS commits other currencies to keeping down the D-Mark, thus harming their economies and keeping German exports ever stronger. That, indeed, is why the French and Italian growth rates have slowed down so disastrously since they went into the EMS. The EMS, like the CAP, is a selfish EEC device which is damaging to the rest of the world, of no great benefit to Europe, and none at all to Britain.

The main benefit of the EMS in the eyes of central bankers is that it keeps the politicians in line. Indeed, the Governor of the Belgian Reserve Bank openly avowed this to the Treasury Select Committee when they enquired into the issue. In Britain, finance is already too powerful, the central bank too dominant. We need to subject both to democratic government, provided that government pursues sensible economics. It is not yet clear whether we will join. Nigel Lawson and the Treasury, the media and the CBI want to; Mrs Thatcher doesn't. The outcome of the struggle is unpredictable. Mrs Thatcher is strong, but right for the wrong reasons and may well be prevailed on to join as a counter in negotiations, or as the price for the single market and the deregulation she wants: the smooth men may yet win against the hairy woman.

Yet entry would be disastrous. Britain would go in at too high a rate; past history and the attitudes of a Tory government, which has always kept sterling overvalued and is now desperate to keep it so and might welcome EMS help to that end, tell us that. Notice, for instance, the unchanging chorus saying that each rate against the D-Mark as we rose from 2.80 to 3.00 to 3.20 is the 'right' rate. They don't know and would accept any rate. As for our competitors who would have a say, they would opt for high sterling to sustain their access to our market. Then every instrument of policy and particularly interest rates would have to be geared to sustaining the rate. Yet because our inflation rate is always higher than Germany's our interest rates would be correspondingly higher. So money would flow in on deposit between revaluations which are only occasional under a managed regime, making it difficult to hold sterling in its bands and requiring internal deflation. As realignment approached – and it would be much more predictable than outside the mechanism – the money flows would suddenly be reversed, seeking refuge in Germany until it was time to come back. The result would be ever rising interest rates and a one-way bet for speculators who are guaranteed against loss by the central banks, also known as the taxpayer.

Britain would have abandoned control of its own rate as an instrument of national policy. Everything would have to be geared to getting our economy down to Germany's unnaturally low inflation rate to maintain parities. Small wonder that the EMS has turned Europe into the slow growth/high unemployment black spot of the world. It slowed Italy down and would certainly break us. It would make Labour's job impossible – similar to that in Mitterrand's France when expansion had to be choked back to keep France in the EMS. M. Delors went off to get his reward in Brussels and the Socialists were defeated. The devaluation necessary as Labour came in to power would be far more difficult and could not be fixed to suit our purposes. We would, of course, find it easier to hold down the rate as members. Indeed, the only case for joining would be after a massive devaluation by an incoming government which then joined the EMS to stop the pound rising. Yet this would mean using it for our purposes, and neither that nor the sustained undervaluation needed would be acceptable to the other members.

The first step of an incoming Labour government dedicated to expansion must be devaluation, substantial and immediate, akin to that carried out by expansionary Socialist governments in Sweden (16 per cent devaluation), Australia (10 per cent) and New Zealand (20 per cent). The blame can then be put where it belongs, on the outgoing government, and the issue got out of the way. Labour must never again come in and attempt to earn the gratitude of the financial community by a fruitless struggle to maintain the pound at an untenable level. There can be no Socialism, no expansion, no Keynesian management of the economy without a competitive currency. To try to hold the line where the present government leaves it repeats the failures of both the Wilson government in 1964 and the Mitterrand government in France from 1981 to 1982. A long and discrediting struggle against the inevitable means being forced into betrayal of everything Socialism stands for, as well as ultimate failure. Finance loves Labour to work for it and be ruined in the process. And this has happened to every Labour government except that of 1923, which wasn't in power long enough.

Devaluation must be a central part of any expansionary strategy. It announces that the economy is to be run for industry not finance. It gives both domestic and foreign buyers an incentive to buy British goods by pricing them back into markets. It provides the insulation which tariffs provided in the thirties, preventing the expansion of domestic demand which Labour would carry through washing overseas into a brief import bonanza boosting competitors. Instead, competitiveness channels the boost to British industry. In a world awash with footloose money, where imports have such a substantial share of our market and where industries can set themselves up anywhere and use an open market to supply ours with their marginal production, it is highly unlikely that we can stimulate investment in Britain, in productive assets, in opening closed factories and facilities, in expanding production, in import substitution and export increase, in all the things necessary to put our people back to work, until the threat from imports and their growing dominance is eased. Unless this is done why invest in Britain?

The devaluation must be substantial. This signals government's intentions and makes growth the central priority. It puts Labour in charge of the high – or perhaps low – ground. But it's no use thinking, as Labour does with its traditional penchant for half-baked compromises, of the kind of two-stage devaluation we envisaged in 1983. We have to outbid finance and the money market rather than leave ourselves at their mercy. They have proclaimed, and always will when it is supported by high interest rates, their confidence in the current exchange rate. The higher it is, the more it suits them. With Labour in power they would be happy to speculate on a fall in the rate if they were allowed. It may be unpatriotic and derogatory to sterling but it makes sense (and profit) to them. So Labour must undercut that inevitable bid against it by bringing the rate down to a level where they have no alternative but to bid it up.

Secondly, the devaluation must also be sustained. Government has to provide competitiveness and pledge to maintain it. Without that guarantee every bet will be hedged, investment will not take place, factories will not be reopened or built for our timid capitalism needs a guarantee that it is worthwhile replacing imports or building for exports. Confidence is crucial. Only the knowledge that Britain has become, and will remain, a competitive base for industry, gearing all its policies to industry and growth, will create and sustain expansion. Growth is a self-fulfilling prophecy. Government's part of the bargain is to provide and maintain competitiveness.

Labour must be absolutely clear headed about the policy and know exactly what it is going to do, and do it. The public face can be more coy and equivocal, as it was in both Sweden and New Zealand. There Socialists made up their minds well before coming to power that they could only escape from their traps by devaluation but kept quiet about it until they actually did it. It's no use frightening people more than we do already by actually emblazoning it on the masthead. Just know it will be done and keep mum.

If mentioned at all, it is better talked of as 'boosting Britain', 'cheap money' or 'making money work for people'. We do not even need to include it in the manifesto. The prospect of Labour's advent to government will bring the exchange rate down. The problem will be to keep it down, not to hold it up. Those who talk of a free fall realise neither how far the rate needs to fall nor the strength of the safety net. Bottomless fall is a myth to frighten radicals and other old ladies. The currency of a major economy with oil reserves, overseas investments, and an industrial sector becoming more powerful and competitive with every fall in the exchange rate, is unlikely to overshoot. In the American case, each improvement in the balance of payments brought about by the fall of the dollar has produced an unwanted rise in the dollar. Competitors want it up, as they will ours, because otherwise they prepare a rod for their own backs. We have been helping them all these years when we need to resist them.

Competitiveness is what we want and what we would get. Financial opinion would bring the pound down. Accept their offer or outbid it as necessary by specifying the preferred rate and use the machinery of management to sustain it. Lemmings can be a Labour saving device. The necessary fall is indicated by comparing present exchange rates with the last quarter of 1976. We were not especially competitive then, but undertook to the IMF to keep our manufactures competitive, so the rate then had an authoritative endorsement. Despite this, on 12 August 1988, the ratio of export to import prices for finished manufactures had risen 35 per cent to an all-time high and our export prices had risen in real terms by 37 per cent. The rate against the D-Mark – at DM 3.22 – was up 45 per cent against the dollar – $1.71 – up 30 per cent. All the sacrifices of closures and redundancy, all the gains in productivity and efficiency since 1976, are in vain in the face of that crippling burden.

British industry has been running faster, not even to stand still but to slip back four-tenths.

The freeze, squeeze and wage cuts necessary to make good that overvaluation by deflation would make 1979–81's amateur Armageddon look like a Sunday school picnic. Losing ground is easy; winning it back is more expensive. New dealer networks have to be established, new capacity installed, new suppliers organised, new factories built, and new workers trained. In uncertainty firms wait and see, particularly the British. Once bitten, several per cent shy, so a badly battered industry has to be bribed by a risk premium to persuade it to take on costs which are greater still in a highly competitive world. When our rivals started, mostly with a margin of around a quarter over us, world trade was expanding rapidly. Today's slower expansion requires a bigger margin to break back in and to lure investors to put up the money to produce the tens of thousands of products we used to make but now don't.

The devaluation needs to be in the region of a third or more. If the pound falls by that amount or lower, accept it and put the blame where it belongs. If it doesn't, sell pounds until it reaches the necessary low. With that degree of competitiveness secured, the proper measure to retain it is not the nominal exchange rate, nor even the real one, but performance. The IMF provides relative export unit values, the prices our goods trade at, but these are published only after a delay of many months. The best continuous guide is the monthly figures for the UK terms of trade for finished manufactures, an instant guide to the competitive health of British industry. Economic management must be geared to maintain these at a competitive (i.e. low) figure on a sustained basis. Prolonged overvaluation requires a prolonged period of undervaluation to compensate and the prolongation is crucial because British industry is programmed to caution, born of complacency, heightened by fear. It needs a raging boom to push it to invest. Even then it only does so grudgingly, responding too late with too little. Bottle-necks in skills, supplies, space, equipment have to become positively constricting before they are broken. Only a prospect which is both so overwhelming that it cannot be ignored and shimmering into the distance will boost the investment necessary to expand production, build new plants and grow to scale – as distinct from just saving labour, business's highest aspiration under Thatcherism.

In the 1964–6 National Plan, high hopes were generated and huge efforts invested in a strategy for 3.8 per cent annual growth. Sectoral and regional planning councils mobilised industry, goodwill emerged, only to have the whole effort aborted by Harold

Wilson's instinctive response of 'protect sterling' rather than 'sustain growth' in July 1966. The possibility of such a betrayal must be eliminated. Ministers must lock themselves to growth and competitiveness and eat the key, rather than their own words. Expansion sucks in imports, particularly machine tools, production goods and raw materials, rather than manufactures which could be made here. Such balance of payments problems, the real 'problems of success', actually help because they keep the pound down. Opportunities from expanding the home market are in inverse ratio to the size of the payments problems.

Cheap money too keeps the pound down and puts money to work for the people. Nigel Lawson's view of interest rates is 'when I think they ought to go up, they go up, and when I think they should come down, they come down' – a much more candid statement than his earlier coy disclaimers, and appropriate too. They are his only lever for managing the economy, though he misuses them to keep them high when UK interest rates should be lower than others because we have more idle resources. So keep MLR at a low rate calculated to boost investment and hold the pound down. If the City tries to bid it up, as they did in 1978, call their bluff by printing money.

An increase in the number of jobs requires a corresponding increase in spending. Unless domestic credit is allowed to expand, an increase in spending will reduce saving, increasing the cost of holding money. Only a massive increase in the money supply can stop this. Thus the proper critique of this government's credit expansion is not its scale, but the fact that it is so lopsidedly private, so unregulated and so heavily directed to asset speculation and consumption rather than production and investment. Government was handing much of the running of the economy to the merchants of greed and the banks, both of whom did well out of it. Consumer borrowing which grows at 20 per cent a year also wins elections, and the Bank of England's laxity in 1983 and 1987 was in marked contrast to its stringency in 1970 and 1979, when Labour was seeking re-election (Table 6).

Public sector investment was being cut, private credit was

Table 6 Credit and Elections

	M3	Domestic Credit Expansion
1.3.78–31.3.79	+£ 7,870m	+£ 9,800
1.1.82–31.3.83	+£12,040m	+£22,200
1.1.86–31.3.87	+£34,015m	Not published

allowed to roar ahead. The negative 1988–9 PSBR, repaying some £12 billion in public sector borrowing, is likely to be accompanied by an increase of at least £40 billion in sterling M3. In the year ending July 1988, the banks had printed £36 billion of new money increasing the total to 267 per cent above the level in the second quarter of 1979, all making capital assets dearer instead of widening and deepening them. The high rate of interest – 12 per cent as against 5 per cent in West Germany – was clear proof that credit was far too tight. The only consolation was that the credit explosion did at least show that a massive increase in the money supply did not boost inflation. It can hardly be argued that public credit is inflationary when private isn't.

Printing money is not original sin. All money is 'printed money'. In July 1988, no less that £143 billion had been 'printed' since May 1979, measured in terms of sterling M3. All was for private profit, none for the benefit of the nation. Government has borrowed more than it needed to finance the PSBR, returning the surplus to the private sector and saddling the taxpayer with long-term debt at punitive rates of interest. Labour spends too much time moralising about the evils of credit and not enough understanding it. Credit is leverage. If working people can use it to improve their lot, under proper regulation to prevent exploitation, and with lower interest rates to cut their tribute to wealth, it should be encouraged – provided credit is fairly spread. Expansionary government requires the fuel of money flowing from public and private sources, banks and gilts, credit cards and national savings out to people and their purposes. One man's spending is another man's income, so increasing spending means increasing jobs. What is required is more and cheaper money, better managed credit to channel it directly to jobs, plus the supplementing of private credit by the use of the state's power for common purposes. Money created is spent to increase demand and tax revenues, sent overseas to bring down sterling, or saved to bring down interest rates and inflation – all benign purposes and none of them inflationary so long as there are idle resources.

The test is jobs. We need them from all sources: public works, services, manufacturing, and however financed, whether by public or private spending, or even tax cuts. Any increase in disposable incomes can trigger an increase in demand, and reductions in taxation and increases in benefits are also bargaining counters to discourage cost–push inflation. The balance between tax reductions and increases in social security benefits should be determined by the shortfall in spending, and targeted to help those who spend quickly rather than save; just the groups who need help anyway. Subject to this, the more that is saved or spent the better. Saving brings down interest rates. Private spending makes itself felt much faster than public spending.

The problem is not the amount of money pumped into the economy. The last Labour government reduced the money stock by 29 per cent in real terms, a squeeze without precedent. The Conservatives have allowed it to expand by over 70 per cent, but still less than is required to keep the economy expanding. This deficiency has to be reversed by pumping out at least another £50 billion into the economy to accommodate both growth and the reduction in the velocity of circulation needed to bring down interest rates and the exchange rate. Government credit is as effective here as bank credit and probably cheaper, such is the power of the state. Because that power is not being used Britain is underborrowed compared to competitors, and to that degree underrun. The problem is how best to direct it. Government credit is readily directed but expansion also requires control over private credit. The answer is to reverse the whole post-war trend towards ever looser control over credit.

If government's only economic regulator is interest rates and the consumer is impervious to increases, the pound is pushed up, industry is punished and domestic growth checked, all to no purpose. Government dare not reduce interest rates for fear of adding to the credit problem. The car is driven with brakes on hard because the accelerator is jammed down, a driving method which damages the engine but is inevitable for those with an ideological prejudice against steering wheels as a means of managing the market. Control of credit can channel it where it is most needed (and presently least available) to industry, investment, jobs, building economic strength. Abandoning it to market forces means sacrificing the interests of the real to the money economy and its priorities, which are not those of the nation. Borrowing money for asset speculation yields a higher return than long-term investment in wealth creation and so syphons money away from it. Thus the end result is an economy totally dependent on overseas money flows. In an open economy, monetary policy governs the external balance and fiscal policy the internal. The fiscal weapon is by far the most effective because it reduces domestic demand and the pound and helps exports, yet since this government declines to use it to manage demand, and since the level of interest rates is largely driven by the movement of international capital on which we have made ourselves totally dependent by damaging industry so badly, monetary policy is largely determined by those same flows too. This takes it out of the hands of government and makes its policies subject to veto by the central bank and international financial opinion – just as it was before 1931. The new economic liberalism has reduced us to the old dependence but with a much weaker economy.

What is needed to ensure that the increase in credit, which Labour as well as the Tories will need, is used to benefit the real economy are effective controls over the use to which credit is put. In the post-war era, with the nationalisation of the Bank of England and a financial community conditioned to following government directions, that degree of control over credit existed. The Conservative government of the fifties edged away from it, preferring, as a party representing money, management by higher interest rates. The theory was (and is) that by restraining the propensity to borrow they could control both the money supply and demand. This was always a doubtful proposition. It is no longer tenable in the eighties when consumer credit demand is largely impervious to interest rate rises, and asset appreciation, particularly in house prices, means that it pays to borrow as long as the inflation goes on. Higher interest rates bring money pouring in from overseas, increasing the money supply and encouraging domestic bonanzas by borrowing even more, thus stoking up the asset inflation because the price of houses, property and land depend on the availability of finance. As a result the supply of money increases as the price of money rises; a supply-driven money stock growth which, in turn, justifies ever higher interest rates, higher sterling, more money coming in and industrial ruin. High interest rates are built in and with them comes short-term thinking. A society crippled by high interest rates does not invest for the future but relies on the asset inflation of what it has already. It becomes dependent on finance and money rather than production and those who create and is a society of institutionalised decline. The knot has to be cut through. The 1958 Radcliffe Committee Report, *The Monetary and Credit System*, suggested the way. Regulatory action should be directed at bank advances and strengthened by a provision automatically restricting advances in relation to deposits received, which is preferable to placing an absolute limit on the amount of money advanced. The Radcliffe advice was ignored at the time, but we should heed it now.

From time to time, as from April 1960 to November 1962 or April 1965 to September 1971, the Bank of England called for Special Deposits. At one time these reached a peak of 3 per cent of gross receipts. This was then replaced by a new scheme of interest-bearing deposits from all banks, reinforced from December 1971 by non-interest-bearing supplementary deposits – the 'corset' – which penalised with increasing severity those banks which allowed their eligible interest-bearing liabilities to increase at a rate in excess of the maximum laid down by the Bank.

The Wilson government of 1964–70 also relied on direct intervention in the form of notices to the banks, backed, in June 1968, by sanctions reducing the interest rate on Special Deposits. This was not, however, to the liking of either banks or the Bank of England. In 1970, their proposals on 'Competition and Credit Control' swept the whole structure away facilitating the credit explosion – and the asset inflation – of 1972–3; the first demonstration that asset inflation is supply driven. That phenomenon was the basic flaw in the Heath dash for growth, producing many of its inflationary consequences.

This left only the corset, removed together with exchange control in 1979 on the grounds that offshore alternatives made control of domestic credit irrelevant. The real problem is still whether controls achieve their purpose. The explosion of credit which took place when the corset was removed suggested that they did. Indeed, the corset could have been made even more effective by basing control on the level of advances which are impossible to hide. This is the line which new controls should take. Banks need a licence to operate. They would put themselves in jeopardy if they tried to cheat controls geared to the level of their advances and enforced by deposits with the Bank of England. This does not cover offshore operations. Yet they can be dealt with by a tax on borrowing by companies from other than licensed deposit takers, making such loan agreements unenforceable at law and by an interest equalisation tax on foreign borrowing, similar to that used in the USA in the sixties. The reimposition of exchange control would, of course, cover the same point. However, that will push the pound up in a way an expansionary government would not want, so it has to be a reserve power and not the prime one.

Expansion requires selective control of credit achieved by requiring banks and other lending institutions, including building societies, to deposit variable cash reserves at the Bank of England which reflect the quality as well as the quantity of their lending. These reserves would be proportionate to the loans for both specified and non-specified purposes and designed to penalise the latter. They would be without benefit of interest, a penalty the lender would pass on to his customers in the form of higher interest charges on those non-specified objectives which government is anxious to control. This would create an effective incentive to lend for appropriate purposes. It would also encourage banks to finance industry and its investment plans to the degree that their counterparts in Japan and Germany both do. It would gear the credit system to the purposes of industry instead of using it, as now, to punish industry for the credit excesses, the inflationary pressures and the follies of others over which industry has no control.

Control of credit would be bitterly resisted by the Bank of England on behalf of its friends in the City. The absence of control increases bank profits whereas its presence would cream off those profits for the benefit of the Exchequer in the interest-free deposits on which the government can draw for finance. But it is not new, it merely restores muscles currently wasting and checks banking irresponsibility. Deposit ratios have fallen from 28 per cent in the sixties to 7 per cent giving them even more lending power. They no longer have any requirement to invest in gilt-edged securities, so they can lend even more. The taxpayer pays ever higher interest rates on borrowing for public purposes just to damp down the excess of private credit by government overfunding. Meanwhile, the banks, relieved of any responsibility for the real economy, have poured money into consumer demand, developing country debt (where much has to be written off), takeovers and other purposes whose benefit to Britain is doubtful.

The objection to controls has been that they can be circumvented by overseas borrowing. Yet overseas debts incurred in this way can be deterred by making the terms unenforceable in British courts after a due date, and exchange controls can be reimposed not just on outflows but both ways. This could be circumvented yet it did act as a major restraint and though a lot of horses have bolted, reimposition would close the door to a lot more and to private inflows pushing the pound up. Prudence requires the restoration at least of the framework so that controls can be kept as a weapon in reserve. An expansionary government may need it in the unlikely event that international capital attempts to stop Britain escaping from its clutches. It will get its fingers burnt but the knowledge that a flame thrower is available might be a deterrent.

Public credit is more easily directed to the purposes of expansion and the real economy. The policy of reducing debt can be reversed as need be, but increases in government spending on goods and services have less effect on employment if financed by increased borrowing, or taxation, than if credit is created. Increased taxation reduces the spending of those who are taxed, increased government borrowing raises interest rates and/or reduces investment elsewhere in the community. So borrowing won't be an exclusive answer and not all the debt will be funded. Government did not fund it in the 1930s, neither does it do so in war. So why do so now?

The banks could also be required to hold more of their assets in gilt-edged securities as they did in the thirties, transferring power, and money, from them to the state. Treasury Bills are now only a tiny fraction of borrowing compared to fifty years ago, so issuing more allows the banks to enjoy their benefits and government to fund more of its debt this way. We can also pay government bills for specific purposes by Bank of England cheques issued on the instruction of government. The credit power of our Reserve Bank deserves to be used just as much as that of the private banks.

Mastering money, creating it, spreading it, using it, is putting it at the service of the people rather than the institutions. Protests will come from those who believe in the quantity theory of money or own lots of it, for both see a democracy as a threat, inflation as a consequence, and the two as anathema. In fact money has to be both well spread and well used if it is to work for growth, not selfishness.

The relationship between money and the economy is like that between water and plant; endogenous not exogenous. The economy uses money and takes the supply it needs. Stop the water supply and the plant dies; reduce it below the necessary level and it is stunted. Flooding is equally dangerous. Disciplining the economy through the money supply or throwing it in in overgenerous indulgence is equally simplistic. The real problem is to manage the supply to match the needs. Meanness and stringency serve only the sectional purposes of those who have, not the have-nots. Err to generosity and in doing so spread it better. Excess is absorbed in a velocity of circulation currently reduced, indicating that interest rates are too high, economic activity too low. Expansion will bring down the one and improve the other. That way we achieve a proper balance. Deregulation has become so fashionable because finance, the force for destabilisation, wants it. The consequences have been imposed on industry, which is more predictable but far more vulnerable. Mastering money gets things into proportion and protects industry from having to bear the consequences of our lack of control over finance. It regulates the water supply to give the plant a more secure environment to grow.

Chapter 7
Manufacturing Matters

British attitudes towards industry differ from those of almost every other industrial country, except America. As the first industrial nation, our powerful industry grew up almost by accident. It has had to survive since without, at times despite, the ministrations of government. In nearly all the others industry was the instrument of nation-building, the basis of national strength, the focus of government attention and interest.

From this background competitors had a realistic view of what industry needs for success in a world economy of imperfect but intense competition between big companies and national bases, where industries and government maintain close corporate relationships. British attitudes remained conditioned by nineteenth-century free trade and *laissez-faire*, both more appropriate to a large, powerful, self-sufficient continental economy like the United States, where so many of our business attitudes spring from, than to a world of competing national conspiracies, each seeking their own self-interest when Britain's economy was fragile and increasingly vulnerable. Industry's highest interest and desire is to be left alone. 'Get government out of business' and all, we are told, will be well. Among competitors that degree of distance neither exists nor is desired. Government and business work together in corporate collusion against the world. The state underpins, supports and works with industry, understanding its needs. It either provides services, as in Germany, or works in closer collusion as in France and Japan. To them our approach seems either folly or a luxury undermining a national interest which is still central.

As a result Britain, which has never really had an effective industrial strategy, needs one desperately. Competitors, having built up their industrial base to the point where it can power ahead with less support, still have one, but are well able to dilute it because industry is more self-sufficient on its own. Expansionary government will close the distance, fill the interstices, and cooperate. It will have an industrial strategy simply expressed as putting industry at the centre and making it the instrument of expansion and rebuilding. Without one the immutable laws of a large open market will reduce it to an irrelevant peripheral failure exposed to dynamics which drain the periphery and focus growth on the population and wealth centres. Academics, politicians, journalists, and the white collar gentility do not like manufacturing, it is messy, strike-prone and dirty. Environmentalists despise it, it pollutes, poisons and gobbles resources. Sophisticates tell us its day has gone, even the Communist Party dismisses mass production as 'Fordism'. It is time, we are told, by the Tofflers, for the information society, chips with everything, and a world clustered round its home VDU. Manufacturing is unsmart, something for NICs who know no better, and in leading the way to the post-industrial society Britain is building a better future.

All this is idealistic and self-serving nonsense. Manufacturing generates more productivity than other sectors. So the price of manufactured goods declines relative to services, manufacturing's share of GDP falls, and manufacturing produces more with fewer employees – an inevitable, even desirable, development but very different from what has happened in Britain where manufacturing collapse is the problem. It is manufactured goods that we are importing to destroy manufacturing jobs here. In other countries manufacturing output is up, manufacturing flourishes. Nowhere has it shrunk as far and fast as here. Manufacturing decline on the British scale, and the resulting rise of unemployment, are both unique. It is only in Britain that manufacturing output has actually declined since the first oil shock, down 4 per cent in 1987 over 1973, compared to a 42 per cent increase in the USA, 53 per cent in Japan, 15 per cent in Germany and 25 per cent in Italy. No other country has seen such a massive closure of capacity or such a heavy job loss. Japan is still adding jobs in manufacturing.

Unless this manufacturing decline is reversed Britain will become a unique disaster area rather than leading the way to post-industrial joys. This government has shown that revival is possible in the bounce back from 1985. Given sustained encouragement, and a development-minded administration, it is possible to do much better than that. If Britain is to survive as an advanced country, it must.

Manufacturing matters for basic reasons. Our living standards depend on it. We can provide a high wage, high skill economy in no other way. Financial services offer high paid jobs only for a few. Other services are low paid. Manufacturing is what we have done, what we know, and what large sections of our people are trained for. Those people have lost jobs. They have gone because it was uncompetitive, not because it was disposable, a symptom of defeat not progress. The decline of our share of home and overseas markets from 1970 to 1988 represents £55 billion of lost output, £31 billion of lost exports, £24 billion of increased imports.

Services will expand. Yet they are not a new economy, free standing and self-supporting. They rely substantially on the productive base of manufacturing. Large sections of 'services' – consultancy, design, advertising, contracting, security, banking, architecture, computers, and many more – supply industry. If it goes, their prospects contract. Consumer demand widens as living standards rise and flows into other areas such as leisure facilities and financial services. Yet consumer goods are still basic and the money flowing from industry sustains much of the demand. The economy is not a series of self-contained sectors. Each is vertically and horizontally integrated with the rest. The sickness of one sector diminishes all. The prosperity of one enlarges the prospects of all. The web of interconnections, the technology, the skill and education pool sustains all.

Manufacturing cannot be replaced. It is job and innovation rich. It supports skills, training, design, and research. Its demand sustains the basic industries of coal, steel, and shipping. It is our magazine in time of war, essential to our defences. It has long generated a balance of payments surplus, paying the nation's way in the world by exports, nearly 60 per cent of which still consist of manufactures. It has a much higher rate of growth and adds more value than any other sector. It is the heart which keeps the economy going, the blood circulating. The new technology, the new skills, the microchip, programmable automation and the robotisation of mass production, all the exploding dimensions of the leisure society grow naturally from the industrial base rather than rising phoenix-like from its ashes. Unless manufacturing is healthy, little that is new evolves, nor can it. It's no use planting seeds in a desert.

The smaller the manufacturing sector, the lower the actual and the potential rate of growth, both absolutely and relatively to other countries. Also, the more vulnerable the remaining industries become without the sustaining networks of a healthy industrial base to support them, the weaker too are the forces of regeneration. Everything has to be rolled harder uphill to move at all.

Where could jobs lost from industry be replaced? Not by services unless we replace imported domestic equipment by domestic service and take in each other's washing. Professions employ small numbers. The financial sector provides only 11 per cent of employment, even on the broadest definition, and is losing its share of the world's trade in financial services, just as industry did. Much is made of the City's 'contribution' to the balance of payments, but 'invisibles' include income from overseas investments, often made at the expense of domestic alternatives and not always wise. The financial sector ultimately depends on a healthy productive base generating surpluses and capital. Japan has it and the muscle to dominate. We rent it, from the past and from oil.

Only manufacturing can bring life back to the old industrial areas. Endless articles on the 'rebirth' of Corby, Bradford, Liverpool; passing Garden Festivals round the old industrial centres like a wreath; are all whistling in the wind unless manufacturing is rebuilt. More than anything else it provides jobs for the semi-skilled, especially those in the Black and Asian communities. It can generate and support more jobs than any other sector – provided we both widen and deepen employment opportunities.

Mrs Thatcher has argued that mass unemployment is the consequence of new technology. Yet Japan has more microchips and robots than any other country, and employment in manufacturing there has grown because it has sustained the old, spun the new from it and kept them in Japan, where we have opted for safety, avoided risk, and lost out on the new – which we now import along with the products, like textiles, we are told should be beneath the dignity of an advanced economy, though we buy them from Germany and Italy. Far from ours being a sophisticated problem, it is simple – failure. Our goods have been priced out at all levels, advanced and basic. Because it has never been as profitable as its competitors British industry has lost out to them, first comparatively and then absolutely, as it closed capacity and devoured itself. Deindustrialisation is the result of that, not increasing sophistication. In 1979, manufacturing invested £1.40 billion a year at 1980 prices, net of capital consumption. Since then it has disinvested, for the first time ever; an average of £1.55 billion a year in 1981–3 and still negative in 1986 by £92 million. Manufacturing is our past and our future, yet with gross domestic fixed capital formation still down 10 per cent in real terms in 1987, manufacturing exhibits all the symptoms of anorexia nervosa. The industries least subject to foreign competition such as paper and printing, and food show low investment but still some increase, namely, 43 per cent and 18 per cent respectively from 1979 to 1980. Those being battered by the exchange rate show least; investment in mechanical engineering is down by 42 per cent and in metals by 41 per cent.

The increase of 1.81 million in the number of registered unemployed between June 1970 and May 1987 was less than half the loss of 3.79 million jobs in the production industries, including 3.17 million in manufacturing. That loss can be entirely explained by the fall in the UK share of home and export markets for manufactured goods. Our share of exports by the main manufacturing countries has fallen from 25.5 per cent in 1950 to 13.6 per cent in 1966, 8.9 per cent in 1976 and 7.5 per cent in 1987. There is nothing inevitable about that. The German share increased over the same period from 7 to 21 per cent. Each one percentage point represents $12 billion of trade, reducing our share by $72 billion since 1966, more than enough to provide jobs for everyone able and willing to work. Our share of our home market has likewise fallen from 83 per cent in 1968 to 79 per cent in 1973 and only 65 per cent in 1987, increasing the share of imports to twice the figure in West Germany, France and Italy. That difference is worth over £40 billion and represents the loss of at least 2 million jobs. We do not even have to recover all the ground lost since 1968, half would serve our purpose, raising our share of MMC exports to half that of Germany and no more than that of the French before they joined the EMS. It would turn a prospective deficit of at least £17 billion in trade in manufactures in 1988 into a surplus of at least £30 billion, a third less than that of Japan and Germany.

Can it be done? We have before: in the 1930s economic policies were dedicated to reviving manufacturing and succeeded. The National Government went off the gold standard, let the pound fall by up to 35 per cent, imposed tariffs on imports of between 10 and 50 per cent, put today's equivalent of £50 billion in an Exchange Equalisation Account to hold down the exchange rate, and reduced interest rates to less than 3 per cent through restrictions on foreign investment and a massive increase in the real money supply. Unemployment fell by over half in five years; 2.63 million new jobs were created; 1.36 million of them in manufacturing. Manufacturing output increased by 9.5 per cent a year to 38 per cent over its 1929 peak by 1937. All this was achieved by running the economy for manufacturing. Some claim such methods are now ruled out, that the world is too interdependent. The paradox is that we can restrict imports from third world countries, but not those from the main threat, the EEC itself, because we cannot restrict free trade with the EEC – indeed, government is busily opening that up. Yet competitiveness and cheap money remain available. All we lack is the will to use them and supplement them with policies as relevant to today's world as imperial preference and a manufacturing tariff were in times past.

The acid test is maximising jobs in manufacturing industry, adding value to our trade with the world. Formulae abound for regenerating the firm: the pursuit of excellence; disaggregation; flexible batch manufacturing; structures open to change: putting the producers in power. Theories abound and some have much to offer – but the problem is macro not micro. Industry can only flourish in a climate for growth, and if the economy is run for its purposes. Here we must learn from overseas experience. In Japan, government policy so structured the economy that the dynamics of growth drove corporate strategy into innovation, and into new organisations for the shop floor to sustain the competition for market share. Insulate the economy from foreign competition and foreign investment, expand demand and provide finance to facilitate expansion, force firms into change, new technology and competition for market share – and bingo! Labour's approach must be the same.

A Medium-term Employment Strategy

Representing money and those who deal in it, the Tories have a medium-term financial strategy. Labour needs a medium-term job strategy to put people back to work in the shortest possible time through an increase in public and private spending and job subsidies. Manufacturing will provide most jobs resulting from exports and even more in import substitution, to supply a growing home market. This is not new technology. We are a low-wage country and it would be folly to concentrate everything on competing with the Germans and the Americans who are at the leading edge of technology. The Japanese did not climb to the top on their own technology. They bought it under licence from the United States, where patents under the anti-trust laws are less restrictive than they are here. We should follow their example. The overriding objective is wealth-creating jobs, not the uneconomic substitution of capital for labour. The best practice now is substitution of capital for labour assessed on a real wage, in terms of D-Marks, currently 35 per cent higher than in the fourth quarter of 1976. This would be far lower on realistic exchange rates, making the substitution uneconomic. The problem is not only underinvestment but its concentration on a narrow range of activity. The industrial base must be quickly broadened, yet on that narrow range we have invested too much in capital, too little in labour. So expansion must *widen* capital rather than deepen it. The USA has done this by creating 15 million new jobs since 1979. There is little virtue in increasing output per head when millions are out of work. Factories would still be profitable at a lower exchange rate, even with less capital investment, reducing the budgeting cost and speeding up the rate of job creation. There would be many low-paid jobs but many people would be highly paid. Margaret Thatcher's failure is that she has substituted low-paid jobs for high paid and lost over a million.

A competitive currency automatically creates jobs by reducing the price of our labour in relative terms, making it profitable to employ more of it, to reopen capacity which has been mothballed, to dig more coal, make more steel and build more ships, where the exchange rate had previously meant losses. It also makes it possible to put up new plants, previously unnecessary, and to replace imports. Everything picks up.

Industry, however, is not one unvariegated lump, to be treated in the same fashionable way. We need diversity and a wide range of firms of all sizes. The front line should consist of the big firms enjoying concentrated production and economies of scale. The middle range will support and supply the front line but also trade internationally, as their German and French counterparts do. At the bottom is a dense undergrowth of small businesses responding to new demands, supplying firms with specialised parts, components and tools, and adjusting quickly and flexibly to new demands, markets and technologies – the seedbed of the future.

In the internationally traded sector, and in basic industries such as steel, coal, shipping and shipbuilding, investment runs are long, capital needs heavy and the rewards from scale considerable, given the confidence and funds to pursue them. In the middle range, programmable automation allows automated batch production and flexible specialisation techniques, as well as frequent style and model changes, and even custom-building to gain the benefits of scale in smaller batches. Fragmented and specialised production of customised products is fast gaining ground among our competitors. That too requires more investment, though less labour, and we must invest there to compete but with the aim of producing investment goods ourselves. Everywhere and at all levels in other types of production, labour intensive is best. Labour should be preferred to capital, a preference which can be encouraged by job subsidy and support.

We must provide the climate in which industry can flourish, encourage it with targeted job subsidies and the cooperation of a development-minded state to help it in areas such as training, research, development and mutual cooperation, and let nature take its course. In an expansionary climate a thousand plants can blossom and grow. If many are less job intensive, and if existing industry can produce more without substantial increases in employment, the spread must be wider. Expansion must take industry back into areas we have lost, replacing imports and becoming again the base for production for Europe and the world.

As industry expands, so will services. As demand grows, so will production. As standards rise, leisure, housing and all those other public services which have been so starved over the last ten years will expand. As the industrial heart beats faster, spending on roads, sewers, public buildings, social and health services, welfare, the environmental services – all the sectors where jobs have been so drastically pruned and provision is now shoddy and inadequate – can increase. A wealthier society can support a bigger and better public provision, and as standards rise it expects it. Private affluence and public squalor is a product of poverty and failure, not success.

Restoring the damage is a gradual process in which increasing the number of public employees in local and national government plays its part, particularly where standards have been cut or services have become impersonal or inadequate, but this must be on the merits of the case, not simply to create jobs for the sake of jobs. A disproportionate number of vacancies occur in areas of comparatively low unemployment. Many jobs require skills for which the unemployed have no training and no prospect of getting it. The number of jobs in the public sector has not fallen by anything like as much as elsewhere.

The same reservation applies to public works. They have a low import content. Our public capital is declining and shoddy. There is a lot to be done, but we must do it with caution not in one big glamorous rush. Public works are slow to plan, engage too late, generate expansion just in time to add to bottle-necks. They must play an increased part but supplement manufacturing rather than displace it in a carefully planned and a phased programme. The immediate public purchasing priority is ordering those goods from cars to investment and construction machinery which boost domestic industry.

Real disposable incomes will be under pressure for Labour's first two years, so the more the public sector gets the less for everyone else, stoking the fires of resentment and stirring up industrial and political trouble. Better to go for quick replacement of job losses in hospitals, schools, parks, manual jobs and then rely on the long-term growth which comes with an expanding economy able to bear a bigger, and better, public sector. We are desperate. But not quite so desperate that we can go too far down the dead end street of buying jobs as distinct from creating them.

Chapter 8
Rebuilding Britain

Ideological arguments about the role of the state, long settled in most advanced countries, roll on in Britain. Elsewhere, the state's role is largely accepted because it has generally worked. Running the economy for growth, using the machinery of state to facilitate it, have delivered the goods. In Britain, the strongest most centralised and most secretive executive power has failed. State power has been used to cope with the consequences of decline, not to deliver growth. So, the most powerful state has delivered least, and because it has not delivered the state looks less successful but looms larger because the private sector is less healthy. Margaret Thatcher, exponent of rolling back the state, has in fact cut back only by reducing its defensive role as sanatorium manager and by selling bits off. The directorial role has become more dictatorial. Countervailing centres of power from trade unions to local government have been weakened. The central will has been more strenuously exercised.

The impulse of politicians is to show determination by structural change, a syndrome which led to the National Plan, the Department of Economic Affairs, the Ministry of Technology, the Department of Trade and Industry – all substitutes for action because none could overcome the Treasury and proliferation of powers was no substitute for a driving will for growth. The priority for expansionary socialism is a firm commitment to growth sustained in the face of all the obstacles. Institutional change is useful not as a substitute for that but only to establish its status and priority. The strongest state machinery in the world can only work with the grain, and using the state positively does not mean an all powerful bureaucracy but a management role to liberate the forces of growth, channelling market forces by enabling, facilitating, and removing blockages. It means as much market as possible and as much state as necessary.

Being weaker than the vested interests built round imports, high interest rates, overvalued sterling and internationalisation, those interests working for growth need a point of leverage in the Ministry of National Reconstruction and Development, a powerhouse built on the non-regulatory activities of the Department of Trade and Industry, with added responsibilities for economic, monetary, and exchange rate policy taken from the Treasury and effective control of the Bank of England run through a Minister of State to make the Bank accountable, as government's voice in the City, not a Trojan Horse for the City. Housekeeping remains with the Treasury, as it does with the Bureau of the Budget in Washington. The Chancellor can introduce the budget and chair the committees on the distribution of public and private resources, but we need a powerful alternative to the Treasury's obsession with the short-term, with candle ends, and with orthodoxy.

The argument will then be fought out in the Cabinet and its key Expansion Committee, chaired by the Development Minister and embracing – through its subcommittees – training, with a major expansion of government commitment; regional strategy, bringing together ministers representing the regions; output, inflation, and investment. Each should interlink with committees representing the department and composed of ministers and officials, so officials do not predigest and predetermine the business.

They should also interlock with joint committees of finance, industry and unions as the pinnacles of a hierarchy built up from the regions, interfaced now with government, not as a separate pyramid outside. Sharing responsibility and becoming the mouthpiece of strategy makes them a lever of expansion, giving involvement our interests have lacked. Corporate management has not failed but was attempted before the TUC and CBI could deliver, and as a means of managing failure, so our interest groups are irresponsible because they have never grown up. Responsibility and discipline can come only with participation. As the system delivers pay-offs and cooperation delivers spending, tax and benefit adjustment, the necessary disciplines should grow. If they don't, the machine has to be run less rapidly, so all pay the price. A policy which delivers will work in a way fair shares of failure never did.

By consolidating the powers for growth and sharing responsibility, the drive for growth can radiate out. By interfacing this structure with the crucial Cabinet subcommittees, the new framework will also provide involvement and influence in the areas where previous expansions have run directly into bottle-necks and difficulties.

Government has responsibility to sustain the expansion: not a premature ejaculation such as the Barber boom and the Lawson laxity, nor an attempt to plan. Government merely provides the climate using cooperation, not control, changing attitudes and providing opportunities through training, education, a healthy infrastructure, inducements to invest and an incentive to cooperate. The market can do it, if it is helped, supported and guided.

Investment

The Wilson Committee found no shortage of finance for investment but a lack of profitable projects in manufacturing. The public has stumped up billions for privatisation, millions for business expansion schemes, and would be equally willing to invest in growth if they believed it would provide the same return. Those who invested in British industry in the past had fingers badly burnt as a result of stop–go and fluctuations in the exchange rate. Profits were low, death rates high. Finding it difficult to raise money, industry has looked internally for finance and with demand for investment low and domestic investment less profitable, financial institutions failed to provide it other than to finance takeovers, mergers, buy-outs, insider-dealing, and the other processes which have made Britain weaker.

There is enough money for investment but it doesn't flow across the gulf between the go–go areas and stop–go manufacturing. Banks, with little expertise in industry, prefer safety and channel money to the highest bidders – property, retailing, media, takeovers – at home and abroad. Even merchant banks, which should be loyal to firms and take a longer-term view, are opportunistic and short-sighted while pension funds take the money and run in bids. All this is in contrast with German banks which are heavily involved in industry and lending more to safeguard existing, profitable, investments, or the Japanese who put their money where government wants it. Lacking an understanding of industry our banks are preoccupied with balance sheets, unable to evaluate risk or market prospects, lending umbrellas in the sun, snatching them back in the rain. 'Wind up' is their instinctive reaction to difficulties. Rather than keeping firms going to garner better times ahead, they take the cash in hand and waive the future.

The Stock Exchange is less an investment provider than a casino, more concerned to spot the next takeover bid than with the long-term potential of shares. It penalises investment or long-term strategies because they depress the share price and make firms vulnerable. This forces firms to act defensively, to do anything, even raid their employees' pension fund, to improve p/e ratios. Japanese and German firms understate their profits. Ours drive up their share price to deter predators and asset-strippers. The nation loses out. British industry has to watch its back more than its front.

Competitiveness creates prospects. To grab them industry must invest billions. To create 2,000 new jobs each working day, year in, year out, requires an assured supply of cheap, medium-term (5–15 years) capital for every manufacturing project capable of standing up to the simple tests a bank manager would apply, had he ample funds to commit at the going rate.

Expansion will need a National Investment Bank to show the financial institutions the way, yet no organ of government could provide money on the scale and with the speed required. So it must be provided, within guidelines, by the lending institutions out of their own resources, with the National Investment Bank underwriting a specified proportion of the loan at preferential rates, leaving the institution to underwrite the rest. Safeguards will protect the public purse by a provision that no loan would be made to any firm which had not committed its own resources in full, including provision for depreciation of existing assets.

Speed is of the essence. Therefore the structure needs to be flexible, responsive and simple. The cost to the Exchequer is the difference between the preferred rate and the market rate of interest on the specified proportion of the loan, plus any calls on the guarantee. In an expanding economy these would be low. Interest rate subsidy would disappear if interest rates generally fell below 6 per cent, still higher than in Germany but the highest we can contemplate if we want a competitive exchange rate. The Treasury would condemn the proposal outright. Their long-standing practice is to treat every loan guarantee for book-keeping purposes as an immediate write-off, financed by a corresponding increase in revenue. This is economic nonsense, so the Treasury must be allowed no say.

Guarantees and subsidies should be funded by the National Investment Bank, competing with the private sector but working with money provided by the Treasury. There is little benefit in bringing funds home to push the pound up when we can create money here with less trouble by using the printing press. The effect on the money supply would be the same, that on the pound benign, with that on the economy more immediate: and government would be in control of the whole process.

The NIB should not just dole out money. It can take convertible loan stocks or provide equity to share in the success of the borrower. It should also be responsible for other loan schemes – to local authorities, grants to persuade firms to set up or expand in areas of high unemployment – depending on the new jobs created and including penalty clauses if that number falls short.

Facilitating the rebuilding would be the task of an Industrial Reorganisation Corporation, acting as a merchant bank, to provide funds, not for takeovers, which have been too lavishly funded for too long, but to allow medium-sized firms to grow from demergers. Competition is a benefit. Diversity of producers and specialisation among firms serve both the national interest and employment. Thus state participation will be beneficial if it reverses the drive to concentration and encourages pluralism and diversity. Since the IRC will have to be built up rapidly, it could be set up by taking over an existing investment institution and running it for public purposes, financed by public credit.

Inflation

Vested interests opposed to devaluation condemn it as inflationary without admitting that sterling has long been overvalued. Yet workers priced out of jobs by the rise in the exchange rate cannot be priced in again unless the exchange rate falls, for as David Ricardo pointed out as long ago as 1820, in his *Notes on Malthus*:

> if we sell our goods at a high money price and buy foreign ones at a low money price . . . it may well be doubted whether this advantage will not be purchased at many times its value, for to obtain it we must be content with the diminished production of home commodities; with a high price of labour, and a low rate of profit.

We can have more jobs without inflation, provided we pursue appropriate fiscal and monetary policies and distinguish between the cost and the standard of living. If we stop being hypnotised by the Retail Price Index we can concentrate on increasing real disposable incomes to make people better off. Expansion is the only way to bring down inflation, reducing unit and labour costs by increasing production, bringing down the burden of interest rates, expanding capacity, removing inflationary bottle-necks and constraints, and eliminating the burdens of unemployment and unused or underused resources. Inflation is there even in decline. The £6,000+ per head it costs to keep people out of work, the burdens of unused resources, of working below capacity with constant overheads, and of ever higher interest rates, all generate inflation. A productive economy makes both money and goods cheaper by generating more of both and spreading them more fairly. The problems are transitional for we cannot adjust the terms of competition to help industry without increasing the price of imports relative to domestic production, while growth produces strains which become bigger the longer we decline, the more capacity we close, the more skills we lay waste.

Import prices will rise if the exchange rate falls. Import prices for manufactures have risen nearly 25 per cent less than export prices since late 1976 and must rise 35 per cent to get relativities back to where they were. Yet domestic prices will not rise by the full amount because importers have made high profits from the overvaluation which has made us an easy market. They will cut their margins to keep market share. UK producers will raise their prices too, probably, but by nothing like the fall in the exchange rate because profit has to flow generously from their lower unit costs. Inflationary pressures do not generate overnight. Eventually, growing demand produces bottle-necks and wage increases, as increased raw material prices feed through, and skill shortages develop, which is as it should be since skills have been underpriced and have to be priced back. Pressures from labour are less likely. Unions are weakened, workers less demanding because high unemployment has changed their conditioning. It will change back, but only with time. Consultation, involvement and participation will offset that process for assessments drawn up through the corporate structure will underline a lesson already understood: there is a trade-off between the rate of growth and the fall in unemployment. Workers who have a say in determining the rate will want to make a contribution to the fall.

Strategies to hold inflation should be deployed gradually, rather than trundled in immediately. Resources are underused. Unemployment is high. Both provide a breathing space and when inflation does develop, the answer is not to invoke a full armoury of weapons to stop it, and possibly the economy, dead, but gradually to introduce counters to stop any inflationary take-off. Subsidies and tax changes cushion the effect: there is money to spare and the increase in output will be greater than is required to finance the higher cost of imports in real terms. Dilution of labour, rapid restart programmes and increased shift-working would help to break bottle-necks. The training programme would build up skills.

Price control would help in specific areas such as the privatised utilities which use a monopoly power for private shareholders. Gear their prices to profits and there is a potential saving of at least £2.3 billion in lower prices and charges for gas, electricity, water, telephones and other public utilities forced to raise prices unnecessarily to fatten up for privatisation or exploit the market. Privatised industries can be allowed a return of at most 10 per cent on capital employed, based on historic costs and enforced by price control. Steel and other capital-intensive industries were allowed a return of 8 per cent when their prices were controlled in the late 1940s, on the grounds that they were risk-free, but the target for British Telecom has been set at 19 per cent to enable it to finance expansion for the benefit of its shareholders, out of its own resources, in effect a levy on existing customers. Consumers should not have to provide money required for expansion. That's the job of shareholders or the market.

Expansion will still need some form of cooperation on incomes. Enter the looming spectre of incomes policy. Unfortunately, this method of boosting expansion to a higher level has been discredited because it has been used only as an alternative to devaluation. Only Labour can operate incomes policies yet we have done most to make them politically impossible by weakening the unions and their more sensible leaders, as we did with the overtough, overextended incomes policy from 1976 to 1979.

That misuse may rule out such a policy in the initial expansion but possibilities open up as expansion gets under way. Probably the most we will get before coming to power is an advance agreement for cooperation in working for targets, plus a commitment to act to stop inflation escalating into an irresistible spiral, particularly in the face of external shocks such as have hit us in the past. Inflation will probably be low when Labour comes to power – it usually is in graveyards. It will be held down by underused resources coming into play and lower interest rates. All that is then necessary in these initial stages is a broad agreement to use 'best efforts' to work to expansionary targets. On that consensus, the corporate framework to sustain it can be developed. Britain then has all it needs, a framework which can grow.

Agreement before the election between Labour and the unions on regular assessments, plus a commitment to full incomes policy if inflation rises substantially, is all that is necessary in economic terms. It is also a confidence-building political bonus. Managing the unions is widely, and realistically, felt to be our role. We were only thrown out in 1979 when people felt we could no longer do it and that Tory terror would be a better way of disciplining recalcitrant unions. The agreement would help to offset any feeling that inflation could get out of control and make expansionary policies look more credible. It would also compel unions to think clearly and assess what they really want, a process which is going on anyway. The unions need Labour in power. Only expansion allows them to do the job. They look for concessions on Tory union legislation. They are negotiators. So let us negotiate. Before power we need a commitment to act *in extremis* and to participate by accepting responsibility and working for agreed norms in return for influence on spending and tax changes.

No one can guarantee good behaviour. Even the toughest framework of control can't stop some employers or employees taking advantage of scarcity or tight conditions. Yet we will not be seeking to stop stresses and strains; the price mechanism has to operate to allocate resources and a rigid framework of incomes policy is neither desirable nor necessary. Expansionary government does not need abstract perfection, merely a commitment to cooperation and participation and a brake in reserve as a confidence-builder. On the basis of responsibility and cooperation, discipline and cohesion will develop. If they don't, expansion is reined back and the blame falls on those responsible, or particular sanctions fall on offending firms or sections by withdrawal of funding arrangements from the state facilities. Unions should also face withdrawal of state funds for their own restructuring and reorganisation. Unions have never been the ogres they have been painted, nor have they had the power attributed to them. They are both weaker and more realistic, and given the prospect of growth they will opt for the future and share responsibility for building it. Once they have made that choice, as cooperation delivers benefits, cohesion and effectiveness will strengthen. The unions will be doing their job: advancing their members and influencing society and the economy in their favour. Both will be run for equity, growth and fairness.

Tax Reform

Nigel Lawson has glimpsed the way: expansion facilitates tax cuts which, as some have always argued, pay for themselves by promoting more expansion. He used them to win elections and enforce his own social prejudices. The example is sound but Labour needs to learn from it by seizing growth to change images and attitudes on tax. American experience has shown that only bold tax reform can defeat the vested interests in the present system. As the economy grows, we should grasp the moment to redistribute the burden, expedite the growth and demonstrate, particularly to our supporters, that it pays and advances social justice, rewarding everyone, not just the 5 per cent the Tories call 'wealth creators'.

The tax system is unpopular and inefficient because it has been used to alleviate the problems of failure. As a result business has been given the incentives a growing economy was not providing, while Labour concentrated on redistributing it, and allowances were given because neither the welfare state nor the real economy could provide them. The tax structure has been used defensively, the burden shifted to people from production. One set of objectives has frustrated another. High nominal rates lead to fiddles: 52 per cent Corporation Tax brought in a much more nominal return because huge allowances had to be made to make investment profitable in the face of economic policies inhibiting it.

Widen the tax base by cutting down on allowances and shelters. Expand the economy, make business profitable and transfer more of the burden from people to business. Expansion will make industry very profitable so there is no need to compensate for low profits by low corporate tax. Provide the opportunity to grow, prod them by tax to seize it, then give the public the benefit.

Advance Corporation Tax has to be paid on money paid out in dividends, but at the standard rate of income tax, now only 25 per cent. The difference between that and the Corporation Tax rate is collected later. Raising the rate for ACT and the associated tax credit to 52 per cent is therefore largely a once and for all gain. UK investors would be able to reclaim tax paid in excess of their marginal rate, as at present, but that would more than double the rate paid by overseas investors not in this position. It would mean renegotiating our Double Taxation Agreements but we could stand the loss in the case of our own unwanted investments overseas. All perks should be disallowed as a cost for Corporation Tax, as well as being taxed in full in the hands of the recipient. The revenue yield would be at least £11 billion a year plus an additional £2 billion in ACT in the first year.

This provides more than enough revenue to combine fundamental reform of the tax-benefit system with an increase in real disposable incomes for the great majority. In 1959–60, a manual worker on average earnings of £705 a year paid only £67.45 in income tax and £26 in national insurance, a total of about £830 at current prices. In 1988–9, on an income of £10,900 he has to pay £2,682, almost three times as much, to support a more elaborate welfare state from which the middle classes are the main beneficiaries. The position is even worse for families. One with two children now pays nearly eight times as much tax net of child benefit – £1,852 compared to £253.

Our parlous economic situation provides the opportunity for

reform. A commitment to full employment will necessitate a substantial increase in spending power to boost demand, to reduce the pressure for wage increases and to make the tax system fairer. This can best be accomplished by suspending the employee's national insurance contribution indefinitely and reforming income tax to claw back personal allowances on the lines of the present age allowance, to introduce a reduced rate band of tax, to reduce the width of the standard rate band and to raise the top rate.

What was once national insurance has become a highly regressive tax on earned income designed to tax those currently earning less than £15,860 a year for the benefit of those with earned and unearned incomes in excess of that amount. It should be replaced – in so far as it needs to be replaced – by a progressive tax on incomes which distinguishes between single persons and married couples. Each person would have a personal allowance of £2,500, increased to £3,000 for the aged, and transferable between spouses. The allowance less £1,000 for each spouse and £500 for each aged person would be clawed back on the lines of the present age allowance at a rate of 40 per cent of income in excess of an amount close to median adult male earnings for a married couple and about half that figure for single persons.

The personal allowance could be followed by a reduced rate band of £1,500 per person at 15 per cent, a much shorter standard rate band of 25 per cent (raised by the clawback to an effective rate of 35 per cent over part of the range) and higher rates of 5 percentage points from 40 to 55 per cent for married couples and 60 per cent for single persons. All other allowances and reliefs except for approved pension contributions could be abolished. Those with offspring would be helped by an increase in child benefit to £20 for the first and £15 for subsequent children, paid to the mother but *taxable* in the hands of the father.

The present discrimination against marriage and against one-parent, one/earner families would be ended in a way which does not add to the gross inequities of the present system. We already have the most inequitable tax-benefit system in the world, but the effect of the Chancellor's proposals for the separate taxation of husband and wife is to make matters much worse by giving only to them that hath. In 1990, a married couple with incomes of £23,395 and £21,905 respectively *after* deduction of pension contributions, mortgage interest, fringe benefits and other reliefs worth around £10,000, making £55,000 in all, will not pay a penny of higher rate tax: and because of the upper earnings limit on national insurance contributions their marginal rate on earnings in excess of

£15,760 each will be only 25 per cent compared to 34 per cent in the case of a one-earner couple with an earned income between £5,460 and £15,760.

Married couples with two incomes can afford to pay more tax than those with only one and the right of the husband and/or wife to financial privacy does not require the disaggregation of their incomes for tax purposes. The parties to a marriage expect to contribute to shared expenses in proportion to their income, so it is absurd to suggest that neither should be given even an inkling via their marginal rate of tax as to the income of the other. They should be treated as a unit for tax purposes just as they are in the case of the state pension and other benefits.

The great majority would benefit from the suspension in the employee's contribution despite the increase in the effective rate at a comparatively early stage. The following table shows the gains and losses for singles and married couples on median, etc. adult male earnings in 1988–9, distinguishing between two-earner households with a wife earning no more than the married woman's earnings allowance of £2,605 (2EL) and one with a wife on median adult female earnings of £7,545 (2EH):

	Median	Lower Quartile	Upper Quartile	Upper Decile
Single Male	483	534	243	−749
Single Female	544	562	515	345
Married 1E	1408	1321	1367	696
Married 2EL	636	661	544	−210
Married 2EH	550	708	317	−205

To this should be added the increase in the child allowance, making it possible to get rid of mortgage interest relief without causing loss to anyone not well able to afford it.

An alternative to outright abolition of interest relief is to reduce it by one-fifth for every 0.5 per cent fall in the rate of interest below 10 per cent. The liability net of tax would still be less than at virtually any time under this government. It should also be disallowed in calculating the rate of tax, offset against investment in excess of £500 a year, and limited to the standard rate. Tax relief for pension funds should be limited to those which are fully invested in index-linked, gilt-edged pension stocks, transferable in full for early leavers, and payable only in the form of an index-linked annuity. Funds would be able to switch their existing holdings into the new stock by offering them to the National Insurance Fund in exchange. The interest payable would be rolled-up and paid on maturity, the income net of tax on the current holding meanwhile accruing to the NIF for investment.

Stamp duty on the sale of dwellings should be abolished if mortgage interest relief is stopped. Stamp duty on shares should be on sale rather than acquisition to discourage speculation, starting at 4 per cent on a disposal within six months and tapered to nil after three years. Mergers and takeovers should be discouraged by stamp duties and/or an advance of capital gains tax equal to 10 per cent of the gain in the case of payments in the form of new shares. Rates should be replaced by a charge equal to 1.6 per cent of the capital value less £10,000 for the dwelling, £5,000 for each resident inscribed on the electoral register and his/her resident children, and an additional £5,000 for each such resident earning less than the single allowance for tax purposes. This would favour low-income households and those living in less favoured housing and/or in less favoured areas. The business rate should be increased twofold or more in low unemployment areas and farmers should no longer be exempt.

The estimated net revenue costs (−) and yields (+), mostly based on official figures, are as follows:

Personal	Income tax/national insurance	−8.0
	Child Benefit, net	−2.0
	Ending mortgage interest relief	+4.75
	End stamp duty on residence	−1.15
	Ending fringe benefits	+1.0
	Reform of Rates	optional
	Total	−5.40
Corporate	Corporation Tax	+11.0
	Advance Corporation Tax	+2.0
	Ending fringe benefits	+1.0
	Manufacturing – reduction in NICs	−2.0
	Manufacturing – loan guarantees, etc.	−0.4
	Stamp Duty changes	−0.4
	Reform of Rates	+2.0
	Agricultural Rate	+0.6
	Total	+13.8
Assurance	Pension Funds – income and gains	+4.4
	Pension Funds – lump sums	+0.6
	Life Assurance – ending privileges	+2.0
	Retirement Annuity reliefs	+0.35
	Total	+7.35

There may be an element of double counting in these figures and overstatements on account of behavioural changes which might ensue, but the tally can leave no doubt in anybody's mind that a Labour government, determined to put the interests of the public at large above those of wealth-holders and vested interests in the City represented by the present government, can find all the money required to reform the whole of the tax/insurance/benefit system without detriment to the real economy, provided it is prepared to give overriding priority to the real economy by reversing the monetarist ratchet of tight money, high interest rates and a high exchange rate.

Regional Policy

Taking work to unemployed workers is obviously more economical and efficient than taking unemployed workers to work. Market forces won't do this because employers do not bear the full cost to the community of housing, communications and other public and private services, and of increasing employment in one area at the expense of another. Intervention by the state to correct this imbalance by increasing the cost to the employer of expansion in the areas of low unemployment while providing incentives to expand in the areas of high unemployment is economic sense. Nigel Lawson's 'boomlet' could have been bigger and lasted longer had it not been so largely a South-East phenomenon.

The most effective way of creating employment in the regions is to increase output in manufacturing industry in ways which favour the use of more labour rather than more capital. Low-interest, medium-term loans for investment in manufacturing, coupled with a reduction in tax allowances to encourage the substitution of machinery for labour, facilitate this. Both can be directed to regions of high unemployment. A selective employment tax would finance a regional employment premium, together with a reduction in the rate of national insurance contributions payable by employers, but only in manufacturing and in the regions. Discretionary loans and grants to finance expansion would also help if made available only to new jobs in the designated areas. They should cover:

1. 75 per cent of specified costs of reopening any plant within twelve months of an 'appointed day', together with a *per capita* payment for each individual job provided;
2. a *per capita* payment for each additional job provided in an existing plant for a period of one year;

3. 25 per cent of the cost of building a new plant or a new extension plus a *per capita* payment for each job provided;
4. a *per capita* payment to both employers and employees for a period of one year to facilitate shift-working.

The provision of medium-term, low-interest loans to manufacturers via the banking system should finance an increase in investment in plants located in areas of high unemployment, because in an expanding economy the rate of return would be higher than required to service and repay the loan. The regional employment premium would help to reduce labour costs and the provision of more 'advance factories' for letting would be a powerful inducement to existing firms, new entrepreneurs and foreign firms. This combination would meet immediate needs. By the end of twelve months, the administrative machinery would then be in place to enable automatic grants and job subsidies to be replaced as necessary by selective assistance in the form of equity participation, soft loans and grants.

Service industries present a greater problem. Extra jobs would be forthcoming if some could be persuaded by higher rates and higher rents to move operations from the areas of low unemployment and leave most of their staff behind. The high cost of office accommodation in London and the South and the high cost of employing labour where a supplement has to be paid to staff to cover the cost of housing and travel are an inducement, but large-scale moves are costly. So there is a strong case for providing financial assistance and 'office estates' to facilitate the transfer of service industries to the more attractive parts of the country which also happen to be areas of high unemployment. The government should lead the way by moving many more civil servants.

Carrots must be backed up by sticks. A selective employment tax levied at a higher rate in the areas of low unemployment and an increase in rates on commercial and office buildings, backed by a capital levy on new office accommodation equal to ten times its rateable value and an annual surcharge on existing accommodation of up to 100 per cent of the rateable value of offices in Central London, will all help the necessary dispersal. The location of office staff is less important as electronics take over and the surcharge would cost virtually nothing to collect, now that Mrs Thatcher has centralised the collection of rates on industrial and commercial premises. The aim of regional policy is not only to disperse growth and utilise resources but to hand more power to the regions to tackle their own problems by regional democracy. A three-stage programme would build that framework.

Stage One One departmental Cabinet minister would speak for each region, representing it in central government and government in the region, backed by a staff to service regional development committees of employers, financiers, unions and other representative persons as part of a national structure. They will draw up, with guidance and help from the MNRD, regional assessments of opportunities and needs for expansion, giving employment, skills, available space and capacity and requirements as the basis for development and annual progress reports.

Stage Two Within a year each region should have its own development agency, like Scotland, with its own funds, in ratio to regional needs as measured by unemployment and the regional assessment. This should handle an increasing proportion of regional grants, working here on its own assessments rather than the initial framework of the existing designated areas. It will be more effective if it can spend and use the money as it sees fit as well as modifying the strategies, for example, by focusing on growth points or using motorways to link the prospects and facilities of wider areas into one whole, the best example being a trans-Pennine strategy to treat M62 land as one.

It will compete for footloose industry from home and overseas, deciding what it wishes to attract, where it aims to lure them, and what package to tailor to their needs.

Agencies will, therefore, get increasing and, eventually total, freedom to control regional funds and dole them out as they see fit, making them the fulcrum of growth in their region. There will be mistakes. Treasury will resent diversity but regions will be determining their own fate, and the expansion will be fairer, as well as better distributed.

Stage Three Elective regional government to which the agency and the consultative committees would both be answerable. This could take over functions handed down from the centre and others handed up from the counties, which should be abolished, dispersing their responsibilities up or down to the districts. Regions should also take over remaining *ad hoc* authorities; health, water, and power, drainage, plus strategic planning. This would give a democratic focus to the effort to develop regions by involving their people in the task. To be effective regional government will need its own taxation which suggests regional sales and petrol taxes rather than income tax, but this is a subject for development depending on need. Regional government neatly gets round the problem of devolution for Scotland without producing hostile reactions from the English regions, for many have as strong a case and feelings of neglect and alienation which are just as strong. Setting them free gives a new boost to growth through regional pride, an instinct which will be just as powerful and beneficial here as in Germany where the Lander are effective instruments in development.

Conclusion

An expansionary strategy which is market driven stimulates development by liberating the dynamic forces of the economy, rather than using the fiat of state power. It will disappoint those who see socialism as the state, those who see government as an assertion of will. It is, however, the method most relevant to a complex modern economy which has been held back, punished and constantly maltreated. To change the whole structure of incentives and motivations would be ruinous when expansion can harness them by liberating growth. The state then comes into play as facilitator, cooperating with industry to fill the gaps between them with a framework of cooperation, support and sustenance. It works with the private sector to do what neither it, nor the state, can do alone. This is not the dominant state, a concept irrelevant in a sophisticated pluralistic society, particularly where public and private have always been kept in separate boxes. It is more the enabling and cooperating state, bringing all the dynamic forces in society and the economy together against the world.

Chapter 9
A Nation, Again

The collapse of Thatchernomics in the Lawson balance of payments crisis and the massive deflation this leads to is the culmination of the long post-war saga of overvaluation, and the nemesis of a collection of quite particular follies of a Conservative government which has learned nothing, forgotten nothing and heightened every long-standing trend to decline. The consequences are horrendous. Imports of manufactures have risen fivefold since 1970, exports twofold. The import share of the UK market for manufactures is now twice that of Germany, France, and Italy. A surplus on trade in manufactures in 1970 of 4.4 per cent of GDP has become a deficit of 4.1 per cent in 1988 and nearly 5 per cent in the winter higher than the USA's in 1987. The deterioration is £44 billion at current prices, more than accounting for the unprecedented increase in unemployment over the period. The British economy is crippled. The measures taken to deal with the deficit will increase the damage. We survive only on borrowed time and borrowed money. The real question is which will come first; the collapse of the government's domestic asset inflation, which has caused and been caused by the credit explosion, or the withdrawal of overseas confidence and a flight from the pound – or both. Britain is drifting, crippled, towards its post-oil crisis.

Now is a suitable, if belated, time for a new beginning. Yet the public mind has lost touch with reality. In the real world we have intolerable unemployment, increasing poverty, an industrial machine too weak to support the nation. Political debate is all about 'bringing down inflation', the 'single market', 'sound money', 'free trade', 'the European monetary system', and other theoretical answers, all well calculated to make the real problems worse. Public men have to talk a certain amount of rubbish to stay respectable. This rubbish has taken over so totally that common sense is no longer believed. We are asked to accept that a nation can have cheap imports and full employment, that industry is helped by crippling burdens, that a shrinking industrial base and national strength go together, that total exposure to more powerful competition makes industry healthy and better provision equals lower spending, while comparative decline is continuous betterment.

The truth is simple, even stark. Britain has failed, is failing and ought to succeed. She can if she chooses between destinies. The instrument of choice is the exchange rate, the key to everything else. An overvalued exchange rate is esteemed as a virtue but has destroyed Britain's defences against every economic ill. Only a competitive rate can rebuild both defences and industry. Few recognise its role: far easier to treat the exchange rate as a symptom or a symbol rather than cause. Fewer still want to admit, other than retrospectively, that it is or has ever been, or could be, overvalued – far better to peddle nostrums than knock away their base. So the left proclaims the command economy, the right urges more market, the communautaire extols the EEC, and the moralists preach sermons while the exchange rate slowly undermines everything.

The exchange rate is the lever to change the balance of power, and nowhere more dramatically than between industry and finance, the real and the money economy. The post-war economy has seen the steady decline of manufacturing relative to other countries, typified by the shrinkage of our share of our world trade, the loss of our home market, the decimation of jobs. This has been paralleled by the rise of finance, the growing power and the worldwide role of banks and the City, the increase in the importance and level of interest rates, the propensity to manage the economy for money, illustrated by the obsession with interest rates, exchange rates and inflation, the increasing desperation of that management as industry declined.

These two phenomena are intimately related. The more governments heeded finance, the more they punished the engine of growth to treat the symptoms of failure. That combination has led to a unique industrial failure, just as the prestige and authority of finance was also unique. Failure worsened as finance rose to dominance. The process culminated in 1979 as finance took power in a government representing money and those who had it and manipulated it, whose creed was monetarism, the religion of finance, which was dedicated to making Britain fit for finance to live in.

The results were disastrous. Oil, a historic opportunity to expand, was thrown away. It paid for manufactured goods to destroy jobs, its tax revenues were used to support those thrown out of work so unnecessarily, while the investment flows were handed to finance to invest in the productive capacity of our competitors. A pointless Hungerford-style shoot-out destroyed nearly a third of our industrial capacity. High interest rates kept the pound at unrealistic levels to penalise exports and subsidise imports, which rose by over half and by 1987 were equal to over half of British industry's own sales to the home market.

For the first time ever, there was a massive net disinvestment in industry and production stagnated. Manufacturing output at factor cost had increased by 67 per cent between 1957 and 1973 but in 1987 was down 4 per cent on 1973, 14 per cent in the more exposed industrial sectors. The workshop of the world was retiring, becoming a net manufacturing importer. Real wealth had increased only marginally, productivity had not gone up in terms of the whole labour force, but the standard of living had risen by 24 per cent in consumer expenditure on goods and services. The trick was worked by eating seed corn. We were squandering oil at a low price in the certain knowledge that it would have to be bought back later, jacking up the exchange rate to enable a given quantity of exports to buy a bigger quantity of imports, selling income-bearing public assets, allowing wages to go ahead of production, because production was kept down to break the unions, using the revenues from North Sea oil to increase spending power by reducing income tax rates, collapsing gross fixed investment, letting public capital disintegrate and run down and the savings ratio fall. Britain's situation was no better for this, except that the irresponsibility of the manipulation turned the eighties into a fools' paradise, appropriately presided.

The overvalued exchange rate was the chosen instrument of Tory government. Kept high by high interest rates, it shifted every balance from industry to finance, from the real world of jobs and making things to the financial one of manipulating tokens. This yielded political benefits to the government; industry paid the price. In 1988, the whole operation ran into its inevitable nemesis: the horrendous 'blip' of the balance of payments crisis. After the interlude of high oil revenues and low prosperity Britain was back in the old trap. Nothing had changed – except to get worse.

Britain has always had a favourable non-oil balance of trade. It has usually had one in total trade. Now, with oil, we have an £18 billion deficit in manufactured trade, compared with a surplus in 1979, a deterioration in our real trading position twice as bad as any which occurred before this government and worse for the year 1988 than that of the USA as a proportion of GDP, in 1987. The Americans met their deficit by a one-third depreciation of the dollar. The Conservative government has ruled this out. The pound, whose overvaluation caused the deficit in the first place, has been pushed by high interest rates to even higher levels. Ministers give lectures instead of help. Industry is urged to hold wage costs to maintain competitiveness, while government prices our goods out of home and overseas markets by raising the exchange rate, closing more factories which would be profitable at a lower exchange rate. This rewards banks which have made enormous profits out of the credit explosion and the asset inflation it boosted, both of which fuelled the inflation. It punishes the internationally traded goods sector Britain lives by, even though it has brought down its unit labour costs over two years; its expansion being the only way to break out of our trap. The current folly killed the Lawson expansion and inaugurates two years hard deflation with long-term decline as a result. We are consuming 15 per cent more than we pay for. It will require a squeeze of 1979–81 proportions to bring the current account back to balance and to slash demand – and living standards – sufficiently. There is no escape and no soft landing. Either house and asset prices must fall to choke domestic credit or foreigners must lose confidence in the pound to choke the inflow of funds – or both. Having pushed up short-term interest rates to attract footloose funds, the bankers' recipe for disaster, the Chancellor has no alternative to keeping them high and going ever higher at each sign of nerves. Pressures can't be relaxed without repetition of the crisis. Britain and British industry are being locked in at present low levels. Comparative decline has resumed. Unless reversed, it must turn absolute.

That problem has been created by government and can only be solved by government. It must throw the levers into reverse to rebuild industry and generate the massive and sustained expansion which will allow it to expand, invest, widen and deepen, and grow. The rise of unemployment in the UK is more than accounted for by the loss of jobs in manufacturing. That in turn comes from the loss of our share of home and, to a less extent, overseas markets. These markets are all recoverable, provided we tilt the balance of power back to industry, make money the servant, not the master, and use competitiveness to get the continuous improvement and growth others have enjoyed, but never us.

The predicament dictates the strategy – not socialist, or Tory, but sense. The real economy has been defeated by its subjection to the instabilities and distortions of the money economy. Every Labour government has been brought down by deference to the interests of the money economy. Labour must, therefore, begin by taking the economy from the merchants of greed. It must run it for the people by eliminating the evils of inadequate production and inequitable distribution which finance sustains. The aim of socialism is to improve the material and spiritual lot of ordinary people, and that means jobs, three million of them, leading to growth and betterment.

Industry has shown great powers of recuperation and regeneration in the brief bursts of opportunity it was allowed in 1985–8 and 1972–4. Provided the shackles of finance are eased, it can fight hard. When they are removed, and the economy run for itself and not for the merchants of greed, our industry can grow just as well as its overseas competitors. Labour for its part has shown the skills of cooperating, working with the unions, spreading growth round the regions, removing the obstacles and bottle-necks by training, investment and planning, and ensuring the fairness which prevents growth degenerating into a short-term grab for advantage. Sadly, it has used these skills to check decline, not produce growth.

Expansion is based on combining Labour's cooperative skills with industry's ability to respond, to initiate the British economic revival, helped by the remaining oil and the confidence buffer of the overseas investments it has produced. Here is our chance to restore the damage of Thatcherism and to make Labour the party of success, not fairer failure. The techniques are simple. First, insulate the economy by using the market method of a competitive exchange rate – government intervening to change the terms our goods trade on. No industrial machine has ever been built up or rebuilt post-war and exposed in a free market to the full blast of a more powerful competition. Free trade which exchanges imports for jobs is fatal. Since Japan and, to a greater extent, Germany will not increase their prices to cut their damaging surpluses, we must do it for them, correcting our own failure of deliberately pricing our goods out of home and overseas markets at the same time, in one dramatic and substantial devaluation.

Labour does not even have to bring the exchange rate down as the Labour parties in Sweden, Australia and New Zealand did. It will fall dramatically and the first acts of expansion will keep it down. The only requirements are that the devaluation shall be substantial – for the financial sector can't be allowed a one-way bet to profit by bidding it down again – and sustained, so industry can have the confidence to grow. Use the market and the price mechanism to give industry the opportunity to expand production and bring down unit costs, and it will respond – unless rigor mortis has set in.

Having insulated to channel the expansion to British industry and not overseas, an expansionary government can expand demand, the only instrument proved to work on our laggard, cowering, capitalism. An increase in jobs requires a corresponding increase in spending, and a deficiency of spending can be ended only by such an increase. The problem is not whether we can spend our way out of recession, but when and how we do it. The deficiency in spending which has destroyed 3 million jobs is due to a shortage of purchasing power, coupled with an exchange rate which reduces the demand for UK goods. The monetarist ratchet of tight money, high interest rates and a high exchange rate which did the damage must be reversed. The jobs were lost as a result of the huge rise in imports and the loss of exports. It needs only a modest return of our trading position and share of our own market to what they were, plus the stimulus of money, to trigger the substantial growth and the breakthrough to new levels of production, capacity, investment and employment which we need.

Money is the lubricant in the mechanism of exchange. The adequacy of any monetary system must be judged by its contribution to the economic welfare of the community by maximising the output of goods and services. All money is printed money and government has more right to print it for the benefit of the whole community than financial institutions have for their own profit. The rate of interest and the rate of foreign exchange are market-clearing mechanisms, neither sacred nor uncontrollable. Their equilibrium rates are those which balance savings and investment in conditions of full employment at a high and sustainable rate of growth. International trade is beneficial only in so far as it enables us to increase output by concentrating on the production of goods and services which we produce most efficiently in conditions of full employment. Self-interest is a better guide to that than all the insights of monetary economists.

No modern economy can be managed without managing money. With control of credit we can bring interest rates and the pound down and make money work for the people, not the merchants of greed. What is required to solve the problem of unemployment is a coherent and mutually consistent set of monetary, credit, exchange rate and industrial policies to increase the rate of growth to at least 6 per cent per annum by a massive injection of purchasing power into the economy, together with a fall in the exchange rate to whatever level is required to enable a high rate of economic growth to be combined with external equilibrium. The economy must be so stretched, and so competitive, that firms are left with no alternative but to add to their productive capacity. As industry expands back into areas it has lost out in, out into new markets and into new technologies and products, so the other problems which have crippled our country are eased: inflation, because only growth reduces real costs and increasing production brings down unit costs; the balance of payments, because we begin to win markets and pay our way by being competitive; the quality and productivity gaps, because we invest, grow and improve; shabby decline, because the burdens of unemployment are eased and growth generates a surplus for public spending. We will be curing the symptoms of decline by stopping it.

Pumping money into the economy advances both growth and social justice. Social security spending channels it directly to need: those who spend most quickly. It allows tax reform to remove the injustices and economic absurdities built in by piecemeal concessions to the middle classes. It also strengthens public control, using the Bank of England to provide the money for investment in people, just as industry uses the banking system to provide it for investment in machines.

The experience of the USA confirms that we have little to fear from a fall in the exchange rate. Inflation hardly increased, nor was there a hard landing. The problem is rather to stop the exchange rate bouncing up as the fall regenerates the productive economy. We can keep money cheap to keep the pound down if we can stop the unproductive use of credit and the asset inflation it leads to. Both are more inflationary than a fall in the exchange rate but can be counter-inflationary by bringing costly unused resources back into production. Selective controls over credit will direct it to where it can be used productively. Government's own credit will provide a supplementary boost in the same direction. Those Labour spokesmen who deplore the credit explosion and urge that it be damped down do their party no service. We advance neither socialism nor our cause by making people miserable. Credit expansion is essential, for we can't put people back to work without increasing consumer spending on goods and services. The problem is that it has been so lopsidedly private, and so badly directed. Our answer is not to moralise but to master money and make it more available to our people, for in a world and a nation awash with footloose funds we can only increase the purchasing power of ordinary people by substituting public for private credit. There is nothing to fear from growth – provided it is channelled into building a future, as distinct from consumer booms and credit splurges – nor from inflation – provided growth is spread round the country, and Labour enlarges skills, cooperates with the unions, cushions the living standards of the people and ensures fairness. As for increasing production, there is plenty of scope to take back our own market. If Newly Industrialising Countries can break into world markets and America boost its exports massively, little Britain can get back too. World demand is expanding, living standards are rising, barriers are coming down. We will be merely adding to our share, and nothing like what we have lost. Britain has weakened herself so far, she can seek her own salvation without making waves which swamp anyone else.

The City will wail, finance will howl, the pundits will chatter crisis, but single-minded determination in correct policies will bring Britain through. President Reagan, the only Keynesian left without grey hair, grasped one simple truth: get the growth and the jobs, and hang the consequences. They will take care of themselves as the fundamentals of the economy come right.

Neither Britain nor socialism has a future unless we rebuild. Decline brings the opposite of our good society: division, bitterness, envy, and intense competition, as the people fight for shares of a shrinking cake. Equity requires growth. The fair society is built on plenitude, not penury, and a powerful economy is its engine. In the end, no one wins unless we all do. We all win only if Britain reverses the decline, rebuilds the industrial base of nationhood and national strength, and becomes a nation – again.